About the Author

Pamela Chen is the creator of the Crystal Unicorn Tarot, a self-published deck for rainbow, Unicorn, and pastel loving readers. Her passion and purpose is to help spiritual entrepreneurs create an authentic, soul-aligned business that stands out and sells out. She has also co-founded High Vibe Witchery, a thirty-day experience for Witchlings to activate their most potent inner magic. When Pamela is not playing with her chickens or slinging cards, she loves to read paranormal romance, travel the world, and eat spicy Cheeto puffs. Connect with Pamela on Instagram: @pamelaunicorn.

About the Artist

Mindy Zhang, aka Mintea, has been obsessed with drawing ever since she could hold a crayon. Growing up, she never asked for cute dolls to play with—she only wanted drawing materials. In 2018, at the age of seventeen, Mindy won the Best Technique Award in the Teenage Drawing Contest. Currently, Mindy is attending Sheridan College for Visual and Creative Arts so that she can continue to share her art with everyone. Working on Witchling Academy Tarot is one step closer to her dream, and she is so grateful for the support from everyone at Llewellyn. Big magical things are in the works for Mindy. To keep up with her artsy adventures, follow her on Instagram: @mintyartz_c.

First Edition
First Printing, 2021

All art by Mindy Zhang
Book design by Samantha Penn
Cover design by Shannon McKuhen

Llewellyn Publications is a registered trademark of Llewellyn Worldwide Ltd.

Library of Congress Cataloging-in-Publication Data
ISBN: 978-0-7387-6219-7
Witchling Academy Tarot consists of a boxed set of 78 color cards and this book.

Llewellyn Worldwide Ltd. does not participate in, endorse, or have any authority or responsibility concerning private business transactions between our authors and the public.

All mail addressed to the author is forwarded but the publisher cannot, unless specifically instructed by the author, give out an address or phone number.

Any internet references contained in this work are current at publication time, but the publisher cannot guarantee that a specific location will continue to be maintained. Please refer to the publisher's website for links to authors' websites and other sources.

Llewellyn Publications
A Division of Llewellyn Worldwide Ltd.
2143 Wooddale Drive
Woodbury, MN 55125-2989
www.llewellyn.com

Printed in China

WITCHLING ACADEMY TAROT

PAMELA CHEN   Illustrated By MINDY ZHANG

Llewellyn Publications   Woodbury, Minnesota

Acknowledgments

Witchling Academy Tarot is dedicated to Georgie bird, my magical parakeet familiar from 2010 to 2018.

Huge gratitude to Leeza Robertson, my mentor, friend, and business partner, who made all of this happen and continued to guide me on my deck creation journey. I have tons of appreciation for Barbara Moore, who gave me a chance to share my unique magic with the world. Of course, thank you to the whole team at Llewellyn for supporting me and co-creating this fabulous deck. Also love to my amazing artist, Mindy, who worked so hard to bring my ideas to life.

Lastly, thank you to my supportive soul mate Anand and all of my friends for letting me type away for days and ignore you. And most importantly, thank you to all my Unicorns for your encouragement and support. I would not be on this journey without you.

Contents

The Witchling Academy Charter

The Witchling Academy of Magic is dedicated to providing the highest-quality education and magical opportunities for our Witchling Apprentices.

Our vision is that all Apprentices at the academy will graduate as balanced Witches with the knowledge and skills necessary to protect the Light Realm against the Corrupt Magic and to seamlessly interact with Humdrums (non-magical beings) without revealing their magical abilities. The mission of our Academy is for our Witchling Apprentices to use their magical powers to spread light and love, preventing Corrupt Magic from seeping in and influencing the soul in this realm.

The goal of the academy is to discover and maximize the innate magic of the Apprentices and help them craft the next chapter of their lives. Witchling Apprentices will activate their unique elemental magic—fire, water, earth, or air—during the selection ceremony and will then be placed into the proper House to develop their powers.

Witchling Academy of Magic provides an all-around magical education. Each House will also focus on a specific curriculum for its element. Witchling Apprentices in the House of Wands will learn how to channel fire magic through their wands and hone their wand-battling skills. The House of Cups will focus on the art of potion crafting while learning to enhance power with their water magic. The House of Pentacles has a full curriculum on healing and growing plants with earth magic. Last but not least, House of Swords Apprentices will be taught how to master their swords, using air magic to enhance their abilities.

The academy will also provide private tutoring on how to build a magical connection with your animal familiars. Familiars can level up your magical powers and are great companions. If a Witchling Apprentice has already connected with their familiar, they are welcome to bring their animal friend to school. If not, there are many magical familiars at the academy to choose from.

By the time a Witchling Apprentice graduates from the Witchling Academy of Magic, they should be skilled in elemental magic and have an idea of how they can contribute to the magical community.

Letter of Acceptance

Dear Witchling Prospect,

Congratulations!

It is with great pleasure that we offer you admission to the Witchling Academy of Magic. Your magical tools approved for schooling will be ready for you at the academy castle. The selection ceremony begins during the high point of the Pearl Moon. Please arrive and be settled on time.

Sincerely,
Maria McNally
Academy Witch Mistress

P.S. Please bring a formal dress or costume for the All Hallows' Eve Ball.

Welcome to the Witchling Academy of Magic!

It is not a coincidence that you've been accepted to this magical academy. There is a spark inside of you that is ready to flourish into something huge. Your unique connection to magic is recognized, and we are calling you to be aware of your talents and to develop them through our academy with this Tarot deck.

Whether you are a Year One or a Year Four at the academy, this magical handbook will be your ultimate guide as a Witchling Apprentice.

Although we highly recommend you keep your magical handbook close to you while you are using your Witchling Academy Tarot deck, it is also suggested that you build a personal relationship with each of the cards that goes beyond the written words in the pages of this book.

Many of you were probably not taught magic, spells, or Tarot at your previous schools. That is why the Witchling Academy of Magic exists, to help you adapt to this new, enchanting world that your eyes have now been opened to.

First things first. All Witchling Apprentices will be placed into an elemental House during the selection ceremony. House selections are based on personality and innate magical persuasion. You will be welcomed to the House of Wands, Cups, Pentacles, or Swords. Each House governs and works with elemental magic: fire, water, earth, or air. You never know, you could also be selected to all four Houses like our legendary Witchling Apprentice Charlie, whose journey you will be following in this deck. You will be learning magic and taking exams alongside Charlie; her familiar, George the parakeet; and her two best friends, Ash and Maddie. You will even help her save the Light Realm by defeating the Shadow Witch.

As a newly minted Witchling Apprentice, you have the academy's permission to start right away! Begin practice on your cartomancy, the divining of cards. You will find magical instructions and your first lesson in chapter 2 of this handbook. Now that you have discovered your magic and learned that you are not a Humdrum, you are welcome to practice your craft whenever you please! There is only one rule: Cause no harm to others or to yourself.

From here on out, you will be immersed into the world of the Witchling Academy Tarot. You will familiarize yourself with each card through a story of magic, love, and power. The main storyline—and all of chapter 3—will center around the major arcana. Chapter 5, focused on the court cards, will introduce you to the essential members of each House at the academy. The minor arcana will be discussed in chapter 4, where you will visit each of the four elemental Houses as you take exams, pass trials, and learn the magic of each House.

Chapter 6 is an extra credit class that you can add to your magical schooling. You will be taught how to create your own Tarot spells. By the end of the spells class, you will have learned the basic structure of a spell and how to perform a simple wishing spell.

Your final exams will take place in chapter 7. In this chapter, you will be introduced to a few basic, but magical, Tarot spreads. Your final exam will be to perform one Tarot reading with your choice of a Tarot spread to help you get clarity on a situation or challenge.

Chapter 8 is your initiation ceremony. You will learn what is in store for you in the future now that you've finished your first year at the Witching Academy of Magic! Will you be a Light Bringer? Maybe you will work in the Humdrum Relations department. Whatever your goal is, you can apply everything you've learned at the academy to learn more about who you are and to positively impact whatever path you choose to journey on in this magical lifetime.

Lastly, here is a piece of advice from Lexi, a Year Four Sword's Knight at the Witchling Academy of Magic. She shares, "Keep working on developing your magic, and remember that practice makes perfect. Believe in yourself, have the right mindset, take positive actions, and you will get results!"

Year Ones, this chapter is written for you. Now that you know what to expect inside the walls of the academy and in your deck, you are ready for your first lesson.

You will be learning all about the deck of Tarot cards that accompany your Witchling journey. This will include what Tarot is, how to divine with Tarot, and a little introduction on how the energies of each elemental House or major arcana card will play out in your readings.

What Is Tarot?: Tarot consists of seventy-eight mystical playing cards which have been used as a divination tool for centuries. The Tarot can help you tap into your intuition as well as guide you to make clear decisions in life, love, career, health, and family. Think of the Tarot as a mirror, reflecting your experiences. The cards invite you to listen to their story and join them on a magical adventure of what could happen … if you follow their guidance.

The seventy-eight cards of the Tarot deck consist of the twenty-two major arcana cards, sixteen court cards, and forty minor arcana cards, which are broken up into four suits. All the major arcana, court cards, and minor arcana names are traditional in this deck and have not been changed. In the next few chapters, you will continue your lesson and dive deeper into the cards.

How to Use the Witchling Academy Tarot: As a new student at the academy, we suggest you get to know your deck and the stories that are shared in this handbook before you begin on your Tarot journey. You will find connecting to your deck and divining a Tarot reading a bit easier if you do so.

As you are reading the story of each card in this handbook, think of a situation or event that you've experienced before that mirrors what is happening in the card. Make it personal and add your own story. The next time the card pops up in a reading, you will remember your personal connection and immediately recognize the meaning of the card.

Since you are going to magic school, you will receive notes for each card. Magical Meanings will represent the energy of the card when it is drawn upright. Shadow Magic will show you the meaning of the card when it is drawn upside down, or in reverse. For each of the cards, there will be a Daily Incantation for you to use as an affirmation to attract the magic of the card you wish to invoke.

If you love fantasy and paranormal stories, then this is the deck for you. We promise you a great time at the Witchling Academy Tarot. You will have an unforgettable experience as you attend classes as an Apprentice and get drawn into adventures, all while learning the lessons of your life.

Preparing Your Cards: Professors at the academy suggest that when you first receive your cards—or when your decks are not in use— you should put them on your altar or sacred space with clear quartz on top, which will harmonize and bless your deck. Here at the academy, we recommend you treat your deck with respect and care. When you have finished with your reading, store your cards in the box they came in, place them in a beautiful Tarot bag, or wrap them with a dark cloth to repel negative energies. You can also sage them before or after a reading. Of course, if your intuition suggests you to do something else, follow your gut feeling and do it.

Before you begin a reading, make sure you are focused and grounded. We have created a mini magical visualization to help you focus and connect to your intuition. If you would like to go deeper with the connection, then lighting some candles or surrounding yourself with crystals can help. Frankincense essential oil can also help you achieve the right mindset before your readings. Dilute frankincense essential oil with water or a carrier oil and dab it on your third eye chakra, or diffuse it.

To begin a reading, hold your cards in both hands over your heart, then imagine a golden light coming out from your heart and enveloping your cards, connecting you to them and cleansing them. Imagine yourself connecting to the energy of the cards through your heart space.

When you are ready and connected to your cards, open your eyes and start to shuffle. As you shuffle, ask your question. Try not to ask yes or no questions. Try starting with why, what, or how. At the Witchling Academy, we like to shuffle until the cards naturally fall out by themselves. Alternatively, you can shuffle them a set amount of times and pull a card. There is no right or wrong way to shuffle; do whatever feels right to you. You can even develop your own Tarot shuffling ritual.

 Magical Tip from Charlie: Just do a basic shuffle and try not to bend your cards. Or, when you feel you are done shuffling, flip your cards from the top for your reading.

Receiving a new Tarot deck is like meeting a new friend. You will have an instant connection of some sort, then get to know each other better throughout your time together. To get to know each other better, questions need to be asked, and answers need to be given. So, to get to know your deck better, you can follow the simple Deck Orientation Spread provided to interview your new Tarot deck. Or, if you desire, you can create your own questions to befriend your deck.

Deck Orientation Spread:
1. What should I use this deck for?
2. How can I best learn and work with you?
3. What are you here to teach me?

Read your Tarot cards in the order that they were pulled. Pay attention to the pictures, symbols, and anything else that stands out. You may first use your intuition to decipher the cards, then use this guidebook as a reference.

 Tarot Tip from Academy Witch Mistress McNally: Read the cards as if they are telling you a story. What are they trying to convey to you? If this was a picture book, what would the story be?

Reversals: What happens if you get an upside-down card in your reading? These cards are called reversals. You can look up the meanings in this handbook in the Shadow Magic section for each card, or you can say that it is the opposite meaning of the card's upright meaning. For example, the Sun is all about success and happiness, but when it is upside down, you know challenges will be coming, and it will be a bumpier road to success.

Another simple way to read reversals is to see if there is too much of that energy—or too little of that energy—surrounding you or the person being read. Say you draw the Fool card reversed during the reading. It could mean that you are taking too many risks, or it could mean that you are not taking enough risks and you need to let loose. Use your intuition and your common sense to decide if you have too much of, or are lacking, the energy of the card.

> "Wishing all Witchlings a wonderful school year. Listen to your intuition and trust your magic. If you study hard, maybe one day you will become the Emperor or Empress."
> —The Empress & Emperor of the Magical Council

The major arcana has twenty-two cards from 0–21. The major arcana in this deck will tell the story of Charlie and her Year One adventures at the Witchling Academy of Magic. Journey with Charlie as she leaves her home for the first time to study magic, eventually becoming one of the most powerful Witchlings to ever attend the academy. These cards represent the big lessons that we have to learn in our lives and the important, life-changing decisions that we come across.

0 The Fool

Daily Incantation: "I am ready to experience a fun new adventure."

Magical Meaning: Grab your flying broomstick because a new adventure is coming your way! Pack your bags lightly, for everything that you need on this journey will be provided. All you have to do is bring your excitement, curiosity, and joy. Our Fool is Charlotte Lee, known as Charlie to her friends. Charlie is ready to embark on a new journey at the all-girls boarding school, Witchling Academy of Magic. She is leaving her home for the first time, and though she is a little scared and nervous, she is excited to see what is in store for her as a Witchling Apprentice. Her loyal friend and familiar parakeet, George, will be with her at all times and watch her back. Charlie is ready to surrender to the Universe and to go with the flow, even if there will be challenges on her path. She is prepared to leave the nest on her flying broom and embrace the unknown. Be like Charlie—enjoy this new beginning. Start or try something new, knowing the Universe has your back. This is the time to take a chance.

"I'm nervous and excited for this new adventure,
but I can't wait to see what is in store for me."
—Charlie, Year One Witching Apprentice

Shadow Magic: When making important decisions, it is not wise to be risky all the time. Make sure you are paying attention to what is going on around you and making the best decisions for the future. Before you jump off that cliff, think, "Does my broom fly?" It is also helpful to get a second opinion from an expert or someone who you respect before you make a risky choice.

I The Magician

Daily Incantation: "I am a powerful manifestor."

Magical Meaning: Like the Magician, you are a powerful manifestor and creator with unlimited potential. Charlie is about to be selected into an elemental House. She has set the intention of being selected into a powerful House. Looks like she's manifested her goal…and more. Charlie has been selected into all four Houses: Wands, Cups, Pentacles, and Swords. She holds unlimited magical potential in fire, water, earth, and air. This has never happened in the history of the kingdom. Remember that if you want to manifest your dreams into reality, you have to be focused and stay committed to your goals. You already have magic flowing through you, and you have the tools that you need to accomplish your goals. Now it is time to take action. Move forward with your inspiration and ideas; take them to the next level. If you can dream it and believe it, then you can achieve it.

"All the Houses seem great, Charlie. We would be
lucky to be accepted into any one of them."
—George Bird, Charlie's Parakeet Familiar

Shadow Magic: Poor planning and unclear goals can cause manifestations to fail and magic to waver. When you are uncertain about what you want or how to make it happen, you will struggle and have a lack of motivation. Refocus and get specific about what you want and why you want it. Let your inner voice guide you, and pay attention to the positive opportunities coming your way. These are clues from the Universe, leaving a magical trail that will take you closer to your goal.

II The High Priestess

Daily Incantation: "I trust and listen to my intuition."

Magical Meaning: Clear your mind and open your heart to your intuition. The answers that you are seeking won't be found within your intellect or conscious thought. They are hidden in your subconscious mind. Let your inner guide lead you to find your most profound truth and connect you to your authentic self. Charlie has been called into the office today to discuss her unique situation of having all four elemental powers activated during the selection ceremony. Academy Witch Mistress McNally is here to help guide Charlie to make the best decision possible. She asks Charlie to trust her inner voice and to let her instincts lead her to make the right choice. Charlie opens her heart and intuitively knows that she needs to explore and develop all areas of her magic. Charlie's final decision is to study at all four Houses and to strengthen her magic in all four elemental areas. Be still and listen to what your instincts are telling you so that your decision will help you find the path most aligned to your goals.

> "Welcome to the academy. Come into my office for a chat at any time."
> —Maria McNally, Academy Witch Mistress

Shadow Magic: If you have a hard time connecting to your intuition, you need to quiet your mind so that your inner guidance can shine through.

The unnecessary chatter that is running through your mind might be coming from the external world or the opinions of the people surrounding you. These thoughts can make you doubt yourself and force you to act out of alignment. To better connect with your intuition, stop listening to other people's opinions and surrender yourself to the High Priestess energy with a calm and focused mind. Trust your inner compass to lead you to positive opportunities.

III The Empress

Daily Incantation: "I give birth to creative ideas all the time."

Magical Meaning: The essence of the Empress is creativity, beauty, abundance, and fertility. She nurtures everything and everyone around her, understanding that great things take time and care to flourish. Empress Sophia is the co-ruler of the Magical Council with her magical mate, the Emperor. She is full of beauty and grace, is the highest-ranking Witch Superior, and is the mother of the Empire. The Empress has worked hard for her spot on the council, and the realm is very lucky to have her as a ruler. Her elemental magic is earth, and she nurtures and cares for the land and her people, helping the Empire grow with abundance. The bigger the manifestation, the longer it will need to brew in the Universe. Prepare to be patient. Wait for the magical moment when your intentions will be fulfilled, and the Empress promises you that your achievements will be successful.

> "This new Witchling is intriguing. I wonder if she is the one from the prophecy."
> —Empress Sophia the Enchanted, Co-Ruling Witch on the Magical Council

Shadow Magic: When the Empress is in shadow, there could be a block in giving birth to a new idea or even trying to express yourself creatively. When this happens, it is time to slow down, take a short break, and regroup. Don't try to rush the process or do more than one thing at a time.

Let creative energy flow to you instead of forcing it. Be patient and you will be satisfied at the end of your journey, just like Empress Sophia.

IV The Emperor

Daily Incantation: "I am a confident and powerful leader."

Magical Meaning: The Emperor is a leader who reigns over his Empire with authority and fairness. He reminds you to have a competent system in place during your leadership so that your kingdom can accomplish all goals as a unit. Emperor Jeff, the second ruling figure of the Magical Council and the loving magical mate to Empress Sophia, exudes raw power. Since the pair came to rule, the kingdom has been stable and thriving. He is bold, powerful, and filled with passion, just like his elemental magic of fire. He has worked very hard to secure his spot in the Magical Council with wisdom and experience. The Emperor is a wise father figure to the Witchlings and Wizards of the realm, and he rules with a firm hand to create order and peace. It is essential for you, as a ruler, to have a clear vision of what you want to create so that you can guide those around you to manifest your goals. If you lead by example and take responsibility for your actions, people will look to you with the respect that you deserve, and you will have a happy, flourishing empire.

> "My fire keeps me looking and feeling young at age 288! I'm the most powerful Wizard, and that's why I am your Emperor."
> —Emperor Jeff the Great, Co-Ruling Wizard on the Magical Council

Shadow Magic: Having too much Emperor energy could mean you are abusing authority or being a control freak. Take a step back and see if you are manipulating your friends and family by being unreasonably strict or tyranical. Learn to trust and rely on others, and learn to be more flexible. You don't have to rule with an iron fist to get the results that you need.

V The Hierophant

Daily Incantation: "I love to learn and gather more knowledge."

Magical Meaning: Magical History is a crucial part of your studies at the academy. In this class, you will learn the knowledge passed down from successful Witches who have already been down the path that you now travel. The Hierophant represents gaining powerful knowledge from your predecessors, knowledge that has already been tested and deemed successful, so that you do not need to start from scratch. Learn from their mistakes and accomplishments so that you can make better choices. Following a traditional structured path will lead you to great achievements. Who better to teach Magical History at the academy than the official historian and scribe Professor Wolf, an ancient red dragon with immense wisdom. History is his religion. He loves to share his knowledge with curious minds. Like Professor Wolf says, "Don't reinvent the wheel. Instead, paint it in your own colors and make it something uniquely yours."

> "History and tradition can teach us so many things."
> –Professor Jamieson Wolf, Official Academy Scribe and History Professor

Shadow Magic: Your beliefs are being questioned. You are unsure what to do because the majority of the crowd is moving in another direction. Learn to trust yourself and follow your path. If you genuinely believe in an idea, don't let others persuade you to choose differently. There will be people who might question you, but stick to your original thinking. You know yourself best, so stay aligned to your beliefs.

VI The Lovers

Daily Incantation: "I know I am loved and cherished in my relationships."

Magical Meaning: The Lovers energy is magnetic, drawing you to a fated meeting with a soul mate, whether they are a lover or a friend. When you meet this person, there is an instant feeling of connection.

Whomever this person is, you know that they are an essential part of your life and your journey. At the All Hallows' Eve Ball, Charlie meets her magical mate, a powerful Fire Wizard Apprentice, Aran, who sings to her soul. You could say that they were destined for each other, a karmic relationship. Their magic immediately recognizes the other on a subconscious level and draws them together, instantly creating a strong bond. When you draw the Lovers card, you know that you are about to find a deep relationship, one you will learn from and one that will transform you. Pay attention to your relationship lessons when this card appears.

"I met the most magical Witchling tonight,
and I can't seem to get her out of my mind."
–Aran, Charlie's Magical Mate and Wizard Apprentice

Shadow Magic: There will be a time where you feel disconnected from someone you love. The communication between both of you will be challenging or may not even exist. It might be because you've both been following different paths and are no longer headed in the same direction. If this relationship does not bring you joy, you should listen to your heart and move on. Make the tough decision and do what is best for both of you.

VII The Chariot

Daily Incantation: "I am confident, and I know that I will be successful."
Magical Meaning: Charlie, her two BFFs, Maddie and Ash, and their three familiars are sneaking out to pay a visit to their crushes at the Wizard School. They have procured a magical chariot that is sturdy and dependable. This chariot will get them to their destination with power and speed. Before you take off at full speed, make sure you know what your end goal is and plan the steps to get there. To reach these goals, you need to be focused and confident in your abilities to succeed. Don't try to cheat and take the easy

way out; you will fail. Create a detailed plan and follow through with it. You can claim your victory if you are determined and dedicated.

> "We've been carefully planning the operation of sneaking out.
> I know we will have a great time and succeed."
> —Charlie, Witchling Apprentice from the Prophecy

Shadow Magic: Things are getting challenging. You may be letting obstacles get in the way of reaching your goals. These obstacles are preventing you from what you've set out to do. There is no desire to move forward. If this resonates with you, stop what you are doing for a moment and think of why you want to accomplish your goal. Think of the options that are presented in front of you. Which one feels best for you? Will you continue to move forward to achieve your goals, or will you give up because it's too tough? It is up to you to achieve goals that are aligned with your beliefs.

VIII Strength

Daily Incantation: "I have the strength within me to do anything I want."
Magical Meaning: Draw upon your inner strength and courage when you are faced with a challenging task. Approaching a difficult choice with patience and love will be your most powerful weapon. Charlie is suddenly ambushed by the Winged Lion, the Shadow Witch's familiar. The Shadow Witch is a powerful Witch who stole magic from other Witches and Wizards for over a decade. She has her sights set on Charlie now. Charlie is terrified, but she stays calm and calls on her inner strength to help her through this challenging situation. She manages to convince the Winged Lion to let her go. Together, they can devise a plan to take down the Shadow Witch. Like Charlie, you might feel afraid, but do it anyway. Know that you can overcome any negative situation, transforming it into something that will benefit you and help you reach your goals. Stay calm. Focus on what you want and how you can achieve it.

> "I will have to find strength to fight the Shadow Witch's control.
> With this little Witchling's help, I think I have a chance."
> —Winged Lion, Enslaved by the Shadow Witch

Shadow Magic: When things have not gone your way in the past, it can cause uncertainty and doubt in the present. The past does not control who you are right now, and you have more strength and confidence then you give yourself credit for. Instead of focusing on the negatives, focus on positive experiences. Draw that energy into the present to help you succeed.

IX The Hermit

Daily Incantation: "I am ready to be guided by my inner magic."

Magical Meaning: It is time to take a break from your busy schedule so you can focus on yourself. In order to defeat the Shadow Witch, Charlie has to go on the next part of her journey by herself. She is led to the forbidden section of the library to find a hidden spell book. When she remains still and listens with her magic, the book finally reveals itself to her. The spell book reveals that the Shadow Witch was always jealous of her twin sister's potent elemental magic, so she opened her heart to Corrupt Magic to gain more power. It swept in and took over. Ridding the Shadow Witch of Corrupt Magic is the key to her defeat. The Hermit reminds us that the answers you seek will be found deep within your magical soul. Take some quiet alone time to hear your authentic self. Let your inner light guide you. Attend a spiritual retreat to do some self-reflection, or find time away from the public eye and meditate on your own to attain a deeper understanding of life.

> "Ah, found it! This spell book will help me uncover the Shadow Witch's past."
> —Charlie, Witchling Apprentice on a Quest

Shadow Magic: Introspective Hermit, it is time to come back to reality. If you have already spent time reflecting but your life is not moving forward, it could mean that you are taking this Hermit thing too far. Perhaps you are so isolated and alone that you cut yourself off from other people. There are benefits to connecting with other people. Don't forget about your friends and family, even on your spiritual journey. Be mindful of others; don't shut them out.

X The Wheel of Fortune

Daily Incantation: "I am lucky and fortunate in everything that I do."

Magical Meaning: The Wheel of Fortune is moving in a circular motion and constantly changing, much like your life and the seasons surrounding you. There are times when life will feel challenging, but remember that it can only get better. Positive opportunities and good luck will ultimately come back into your life. If you are at an amazing point in your life, know that this will also pass, and your life will eventually return to a neutral state. It is essential to appreciate the happy moments in life because they can vanish into thin air any second. The spell book takes Charlie through the different life cycles of the Shadow Witch, including her past, present, and future. Before Charlie can flip to the future to see who will defeat the Shadow Witch, she is pulled back to the present by George.

"Little Witchling, let's journey to the past, present, and future."
—Spell Book from the Forbidden Section of the Library

Shadow Magic: The Wheel of Fortune spinning backward is no fun. This reversed motion could mean that you are experiencing misfortune, bad luck, and setbacks in your life. Don't let the disappointments hold you back. You can choose to allow the wheel to take you for a backward ride, or you can choose to step off and send it in the right direction. Learn the lessons that you need to learn and move on.

XI Justice

Daily Incantation: "I make positive choices that align with my beliefs."

Magical Meaning: Having the Justice card show up reminds you to be fair in your dealings, especially to yourself. Charlie is caught out past curfew and is sent to detention. She knows she has to take responsibility for her actions. Cerberus, a mystical three-headed dog that also guards the gates to the underworld, guards the detention room. He is there to observe Charlie and dish out her punishment. The decisions that he makes are fair and just, bringing balance to the situation. If you are making a decision that could completely alter the path you are currently on, be mindful of the consequences of your actions. Think about how this decision will affect you and the people around you. Make sure your choices are in alignment with your beliefs. Know that your decisions will have a karmic effect in your future, and you wouldn't want to end up in detention like Charlie.

> "Charlie, why are you roaming the hallways after curfew?"
> –Lexi, Knight of Swords, Year Four Witchling Apprentice

Shadow Magic: Are you breaking the rules or sneaking out past curfew like Charlie? You know that what you are doing is unjust, unfair, and unbalanced, but maybe it can't be helped. There are a couple of choices you can make. You can try to hide your mistakes and hope no one notices, or you can own up to things, take responsibility for your actions, and find a fair solution. Remember, there are consequences for everything you do. Make sure you choose wisely and remember the lessons of the Justice card.

XII Hanged Man

Daily Incantation: "I believe everything will work out as it should."

Magical Meaning: Push the pause button on your life and hang on for a moment. No matter what is going on right now, the Universe is asking you to stop and look around. Look at things from a different perspective, like the Hanged Man, because sometimes that's when you'll be able to see new possibilities that may be hidden from you. Charlie knows that the Shadow Witch is crafty, and to defeat her, she has to come up with a plan that is entirely different from what Witches and Wizards have done in the past. Charlie's plan is to sacrifice herself and pretend that she is caught in the Winged Lion's trap. Start thinking outside the box, like Charlie, and find new ways of solving problems that others normally wouldn't think of. Just a heads-up: if you don't slow down, the Universe will put the brakes on for you, and you don't want that. It's better to pay attention and readjust now than to pay for it later, when you are forced to.

> "I hope the Winged Lion gets to the Shadow Witch fast. My leg is falling asleep."
> —Charlie, Year One Witchling Apprentice

Shadow Magic: You've been hanging upside down for a little too long. It's time to flip right side up, stop stalling, and take some action. Quit getting hung up. Stop committing to tasks that are just taking up time and not helping you achieve your goals. You've been talking the talk, now let's see if you can walk the walk. Get your feet back on the ground and bust a move, because it's time to make some magic.

XIII Death

Daily Incantation: "I am open to positive changes in my life."

Magical Meaning: When the Death card appears, it could mean that you are going through a massive transition, much like dying and gaining new magical powers. Charlie engages in a magical duel, a battle to the death, and the Shadow Witch is just too powerful. The fight ends quickly—the Shadow Witch delivers a fatal blow to Charlie. Once Charlie is dead, she travels into the Spirit Realm, meets her Higher Self, and gains the power of Spirit. For you to powerfully transform into a better you, there will be an element of death that has to occur first. Letting go of old beliefs and behaviors can help you welcome new opportunities into your life. View these changes as positive experiences and allow yourself to be rebirthed.

> "I got you my little Witchling, and all the power that you possess will be mine!"
> —Shadow Witch, the Evil Villain of the Story

Shadow Magic: Being resistant to change at a vital time of your life can represent the energy of the reversed Death card. If you are not willing to release bad habits and old behaviors, you can block new opportunities from flying in. This may be why you feel stuck and confused. It is time to shift your beliefs. Choose to say yes to change and to welcome new possibilities into your life. Let go of what is no longer needed and experience growth.

XIV Temperance

Daily Incantation: "I am patient, calm, and balanced."

Magical Meaning: You might not have five elemental powers bouncing around inside of you, but you can still feel out of balance during stressful situations. When Charlie wakes up in her physical body, she realizes that she feels and even looks different. Charlie feels her fifth elemental power of Spirit bouncing around clashing with the other elemental powers. Temperance is here to remind you to be patient and learn how to harmonize the energies in your life. If things feel disconnected or chaotic, come back to your center and maintain order in your life. Don't let your emotions run too high, but be careful not to let them get too low. Staying calm and being patient can help you get through challenging experiences.

 "Charlie's new energy feels even more powerful than before!"
—George, Charlie's Parakeet Familiar

Shadow Magic: When Temperance shows up reversed, it is a warning that something isn't right; something is off-balance. This disturbance can show up as chaos and turn your life upside down. This is to remind you that you might be taking actions that are not in your best interest. If you want your life back in order, listen to the warning, realign your actions with your ultimate goals, and get back into the flow of things.

XV The Devil

Daily Incantation: "I am in control of the choices I make in life."

Magical Meaning: Someone or something has got you bound and is restricting your magic. This is an unhealthy attachment and a toxic relationship. You might not even know that you are being held captive because you are seduced by the physical pleasure that it brings you. The Shadow Witch wants Charlie to join her and conquer the realm. With their magic combined, they will be unstoppable. The Shadow Witch knows that it's Charlie's dream to become a powerful Witch, so she offers to be her magical mentor. Don't let this obsessive need hold you back from being your authentic self. You have a choice: you can choose to break the chains of confinement, or you can continue to sell your soul to the devil.

> "Join me, Witchling, and we will be unstoppable."
> –The Most Powerful Shadow Witch

Shadow Magic: You can break free of the chains that the Devil has laid upon you by confronting your fears and digging deep into your shadow self. Release negative habits, obsessions, addictions, and beliefs. Let go of things that are dangerous to your mind, body, and soul. It might be gaining freedom from a toxic relationship, eating healthier, quitting drugs, driving slower, or even taking more time to focus on yourself. These positive changes will help you take charge of your life and regain your freedom.

XVI The Tower

Daily Incantation: "I welcome positive changes into my life."

Magical Meaning: A Tower moment is when you are suddenly struck by chaos and it shakes you to your core, kind of like finding out you share DNA with your enemy. Charlie just found out the Shadow Witch is her mother, and Charlie's own gifts are the result of her mother's evil ways. It is quite a shock to Charlie's system to know that she was created from the stolen magic of others. An unexpected change in your life can come at you from any direction, including your finances, relationships, or health. This chaos can create destruction, physically and mentally. These Tower moments can be messy, but they don't have to be. Embrace the unexpected. Use it as a way to shake yourself awake and fall back on the path that is right for you.

> "Charlie, I am your Mother ..."
> —Shadow Witch, Biological Mother to Charlie

Shadow Magic: Resisting the Tower moments can only delay catastrophe and destruction for so long. The chaos waiting for you will teach you a valuable lesson, and you need to experience this challenge to move on with your life. Do not ignore or fear the change, but rather step up and face the inevitable. Be prepared for the transition. If you take the leap, it will hurt less.

XVII The Star

Daily Incantation: "I am lucky and blessed everyday."

Magical Meaning: Anything is possible when you receive this magical card in your reading. Charlie free falls out of the Tower with George onto thick, soft grass next to a sparkling pond. She quickly realizes that this is the sacred pond that was rumored to be lost. The water is a powerful healing tool against Corrupt Magic, so Charlie hurries to collect it for the final battle. Finding the Sacred Pond makes Charlie feel truly blessed by the Universe and brings renewed hope to her mission. Have faith, for the Star can bring luck, blessings, and positive opportunities on your path if you believe and listen. Let the Star guide you and inspire you with hope. Infinite possibilities can appear in your life when you have hope. Go with the flow, allow these positive changes to happen, and remember to take physical action so that you can achieve your goals faster.

> "Charlie, look! It's the sacred pond with the magical healing waters!"
> —George, Charlie's Super Smart Parakeet Familiar

Shadow Magic: Are you giving up on the Universe? Perhaps the challenges in your life are adding up and you are you not seeing anything positive about your experiences. Well, the Universe has your back, and you are not being punished. Focus on what you want instead of what you are lacking. Keep searching in the dark skies and, like Charlie, you might get lucky and land next to something magical.

XVIII The Moon

Daily Incantation: "I trust my intuition to guide me to success."

Magical Meaning: The Moon illuminates the night by shining its light and showing you things that were once hidden in the dark. The star essence in the water pushes Corrupt Magic out of the Shadow Witch, transforming her back to her true self, Air Witch Christina McNally. With the Corrupt Magic gone, Air Witch McNally is flooded with all the thoughts and emotions that were buried within her. The Moon shines its light on things that were tucked away. Now that you can see clearly like the ex–Shadow Witch, you will notice that something is not what it appears to be. Before you make a decision, make sure you can see the full situation. Trust your intuition and let your inner voice guide you to make the best choices possible.

> "Mother, your Corrupt Magic is gone. What will you choose to do now?"
> —Charlie, Daughter of Christina McNally

Shadow Magic: Your vision is being shrouded with illusions, and nothing seems to be making sense. These illusions are causing fear and anxiety to increase, blocking your intuition and your inner voice. Allow yourself to dig deep and work through your resistance. Understanding how and why your shadow came to be can help set you free of limiting beliefs and Corrupt Magic. This journey will have ups and downs, just like the Moon's affect on the tides, but it can be a transformative and freeing experience.

XIX The Sun

Daily Incantation: "I am always successful in achieving my goals."
Magical Meaning: The Sun is a card of happiness and success, shining joy and light into your life. The shining light will help you see with clarity and swiftly accomplish your goals. The sun's rays can cast away shadows and doubts, leading you to victory. Keep in mind that it is important to celebrate your successes with yourself and others. Three cheers for Charlie! It is as if the bright sun has appeared in the skies after a long winter storm, chasing away the darkness. Rays of warmth and joy flow through the streets as the townspeople come out to celebrate Charlie's success. Be bold and proud like the Sun. Hold your head up high like Charlie, and let others honor your achievements.

> "The Shadow Witch is no more!"
> —Charlie, the Shadow Witch Conqueror

Shadow Magic: The Sun is a fierce and powerful force. Nothing can entirely snuff out the sun's light, for it burns too brightly to be covered up. A passing cloud may smother the light for a moment, but the sun will always come back out. Your success will be achieved, but there might be confusion, uncertainty, and challenges along the way.

XX Judgement

Daily Incantation: "I am ready to follow my divine calling."

Magical Meaning: The Judgement card will magically arise when you are called upon to make an important decision in your life. This decision will affect your long-term future and ask you to awaken and claim your new powers. As Charlie stands outside the gates to the Magical Council, she is filled with self-doubt. She is re-entering the Magical Society with a new identity. Charlie is now the most powerful being, possessing all five elemental magical powers, even though her powers are still undeveloped. The Gate Angel of the Magical Council appears and tells her to let go of her past and to love who she is in the present. Embrace who you are entirely. If you do, no one else will be able to judge you. The transition that you are experiencing is your inner calling, and it is time to claim this renewed version of yourself and stand proud. Judgement is here to help you let go of the past. Let go of what is holding you back. Go forth, claim your destiny, and fulfill your prophecy. If you get lost, tune into your intuition and trust what feels right to you.

> "Let the past self go, love who you once were, and allow
> your new self to be birthed without a past."
> —Wise Angel, the Gate Angel of the Magical Council

Shadow Magic: When Judgement pops up reversed, it could be a sign that you are doubting yourself or thinking negative thoughts. This is a problem because it is blocking you from achieving your goals. To overcome your self-doubt, be aware of what you are thinking and saying. Acknowledge each negative message and then replace it with a positive one. Let that be your new mantra.

XXI The World

Daily Incantation: "I completed my goals with grace and ease."

Magical Meaning: The World card invites you to celebrate all that you've accomplished and to honor your successes. You have finally reached your goals, and now it is time to pause and reflect on your adventures. You will be able to take your learnings from this cycle and apply them to future experiences, which will help you make better choices on your adventures. Charlie finally made it through Year One at the Witchling Academy of Magic. Look back on your journey and how far you have come, for your magical path has come full circle. Be thankful for what you have achieved. How has your life made you a better person? You have completed one cycle, and you are now graduating on to the next.

> "Wow, what a year! I can't wait to come back to the academy after summer break."
> —Charlie, Year Two Witchling Apprentice

Shadow Magic: The World reversed can mean that the closure or completion you are seeking is delayed. You've been working on a big goal or project for a while now, and you can't seem to come to a successful conclusion that you are satisfied with. Make sure that you are taking action and staying focused on your intention. Retrace your steps and set new goals. Find a way to graduate from this experience so you can continue your life cycle.

The minor arcana contains the four elemental Houses, or suits, of the deck. The House of Wands is connected to the element of fire, Pentacles relates to earth, Cups are water, and Swords represent air. Each elemental House also associates with a specific type of Witchling, based on their personality, energy, elemental magic, and chosen magical tool. These qualities are related to the meaning of each suit. Understanding the corresponding energies and personalities of each House can give you a deeper insight into the meanings of the cards and how they can relate to each other during your readings. They might even spark your intuition, allowing you to gain clarity about a question or problem you brought to the cards. The cards of the minor arcana tend to represent what is happening in your everyday life. They include the smaller lessons you will learn as you move through your day. As Charlie learns how to control all four of her elemental magical powers, you will see how these cards work with one another and interact with the Witchlings from each elemental House.

House of Wands

Elemental Magic: Fire

House Protector: Phoenix

Energy: Passion

Colors: Burgundy and pale yellow

Magical Tool: Wands channel a Witchling's fire energy so that their magic is even more powerful. Witchlings can usually shoot flames through their wands and perform different types of magic, like levitation. Wands will never go up in flames because they are enchanted and made from trees in the Unicorn Forest.

Witchling Personalities: Loves sports, traveling, and anything involving action and adventures. These Apprentices usually go on to graduate as Light Bringers.

Ace of Wands

Daily Incantation: "I have inspiration flowing through me every day."

Magical Meaning: The elemental house protector for the House of Wands is the fierce phoenix. She is proudly shown on the House of Wands crest. The hot, molten-fire energy of the phoenix is well represented by the Wands. Her fire magic sparks creativity, passion, and courage. The phoenix and the Ace of Wands are telling you to flame up and embrace your heart's desires and your passions. Say yes to this new idea. If you have been looking for a sign from the Universe, this is it. Stay open to inspired and creative thoughts, and let them be your guide. Following your passion is the best path, even if there are challenges along the way.

> "Be confident, be passionate, and have courage, for we are the House of Wands."
> –Sandra Flores, Fire Queen to the House of Wands and Witch Superior

Shadow Magic: When you pull a reversed Ace of Wands, it could mean that you have an overflow of creative energy, and it is hard for you to focus on one thing. You are fired up about everything, which makes it difficult to finish one project. Focus on what you are the most passionate about and what is most important. After you finish that project, then move on to the next—or better yet, think of a way to combine your passions.

Two of Wands

Daily Incantation: "I have clear, concise plans
that help me reach my goals easily."

Magical Meaning: You've latched on to an idea or a desire and are ready to take action on it. You are prepared to win. Charlie is getting ready to take action and enter a contest to win an apprenticeship with Professor Flores. She is currently brainstorming strategies to win the competition with George, her trusty parakeet familiar. Teamwork makes the dream work. Make sure that you have the best possible plan to move forward, and take account of all possibilities and potential challenges to ensure your success. Be clear about what you want and how you will get there. Also, leave room for any unforeseen difficulties that might poof into your path. Step outside of your comfort zone, discover new adventures, follow your dreams, and let your desires fuel you on your path.

> "I'm going to enter the apprenticeship contest!"
> –Charlie, Year One Witchling with Fire Elemental Magic

Shadow Magic: The fire magic has been used up, depleted. You are no longer motivated to take action on your goals. If the Two of Wands shows up reversed in your readings, then now is not the time for you to move forward. Take a step back and reconsider your intentions. Is this indeed what you want? If it is, then wait until your fire starts to build up and you feel passionate again before you move on to the next step of your plan.

Three of Wands

Daily Incantation: "I have positive opportunities coming my way."

Magical Meaning: You are well on your way to accomplishing and achieving your goals, and so are Charlie and George. They are so fired up to be entering the apprenticeship contest. Together, they brewed up the perfect plan to take first place. Everything is falling into place—as it should, with all that hard work you put into the planning! As you are expanding and gaining success, you will be aware of more opportunities floating your way. These opportunities add to the excitement, and they add more fire for you to reach your goals. Although some of these opportunities may take you out of your comfort zone, learn to welcome the changes. Make adjustments so that everything moves along smoothly. Let these changes help you dream bigger than ever before.

> "My plan and hard work will pay off. I know I can get the apprenticeship!"
> —Charlie, First Year Witchling Apprentice

Shadow Magic: All this sparkly goodness is coming your way, and opportunities are showing up magically, but you are too scared to step outside of your comfort zone to claim them. Are you trying to play it safe? Don't, because you are putting a glass ceiling on your potential, and sooner or later you will have nowhere else to grow. What is blocking you from dreaming big? What are you scared of? If you figure that out, you can break through the glass.

Four of Wands

Daily Incantation: "I am grateful for all my accomplishments."

Magical Meaning: Relax and celebrate with your friends, family, and familiars. Charlie and three of her good friends have all made it through to the finals of the apprenticeship contest, so they are having a huge celebration. They are excited and grateful. Like the Witchlings, the hard work that you've put into your dreams has helped you create a stable foundation to build on, and it has paid off. It is time to show your loved ones—and yourself—gratitude for making it this far. Cheers to a happy time. Appreciate where you are and what you have right now. This is a joyous moment, so enjoy this magical time with others. There is nothing better than getting together with your loved ones and supporting each other as you achieve your goals.

> "We did it, guys! I am so proud of every one of us!"
> —Ash, Charlie's House of Wands BFF

Shadow Magic: The shadow side of the Four of Wands could be that you are not getting along with your loved ones. Something has happened to cause upheaval and tension in the relationship(s). They could be jealous of your success, not understanding of your situation, or they just might be unsupportive. Surround yourself with people who are your cheerleaders and mentors and who wish you the best. Don't let the negativities of others drag you down.

Five of Wands

Daily Incantation: "I am determined to resolve this conflict in a peaceful, loving way."

Magical Meaning: A Wands Battle is happening right now at the academy, and the finalists for the apprenticeship contest are dueling their hearts out. The Witchlings understand that all the fighting and competing will stay on the battlefield and not leak into their personal lives or affect their friendships. There is a specific time and place to fight, so make sure you know when and where to pick your battles. There is something in the air that is causing people to get fired up and take it out on each other. Everyone wants to be heard and understood. When everyone is on the offensive, no one is reasonable or compromising. If you let this heated argument continue, the fire will only grow and spread. Be the better Witchling and take the first step to listen to others. Put down your wand, even if you still want to fight. Let everyone speak, and listen to them meaningfully. Hopefully, they will follow suit.

"Wands up, battle ready, and fire!"
–Professor Flores, Judge of the Wands Battle

Shadow Magic: Tucking tail and running away? Are you avoiding the conflict by ignoring it and wishing that it would just disappear? Confronting others and being confronted makes you feel uneasy. You would rather deflect it than own up to it. Some conflicts can teach you a lesson and are essential on your magical journey. Stand your ground and find the solutions to your conflicts instead of running away from them and letting them control your actions.

Six of Wands

Daily Incantation: "I am victorious in everything that I do."

Magical Meaning: It was not easy, but Charlie has won the Wands Battle. She took first place, her BFF Ash took second place, and Rina, another powerful Witchling Apprentice, came in third. Everyone is happy with the outcome; it was a magical battle to witness. After all your hard work, you deserve this success. You should be proud of achieving your goal—let others celebrate your victory! As a result of your success, you might receive some public recognition, which will put you in the spotlight. It could be a hug from your coworkers, a first place medal, or a certificate of acknowledgment. Whatever it is, let this fire up your confidence so you can keep going and achieve your future goals as well.

"Great win Charlie, but watch out for us next year!
We will come back stronger than ever."
–Jiro, Rina's Mini Greyhound Familiar

Shadow Magic: Having too much Six of Wands energy could cause the reversed card to pop up in your readings. It could be that you are taking your public recognition and celebration too far, rubbing your achievements in people's faces. Don't let your successes go to your head. Yes, you did a good job, but you need to keep your ego in check.

Seven of Wands

Daily Incantation: "I am confident in my ability to succeed."

Magical Meaning: It is the final trail in the Wands apprenticeship contest, and Charlie is in the lead. All she has to do to win is hold on to her lead, but it will be challenging because all of the other Witchlings are planning to take her down together. When you are on top of the leaderboard, there will always be others who are looking to take you down. Protect what you have worked so hard for. If you can maintain your momentum, you will hold on to your success. Prepare to support your beliefs, and don't let others distract you. Be persistent. Don't let up, even if it looks like the odds might be against you.

> "Come on Charlie, we have to win and maintain our lead in the competition!"
> —George, Charlie's Overachieving Parakeet Familiar

Shadow Magic: You are sick and tired of everyone battling you. You don't want to fight anymore. Why can't they all leave you alone? You are thinking of sacrificing your position at the top; it's not worth all this work. Well, is it or isn't it? Is the reason to succeed still vital to you? Do you still have the same drive and passion to stay in the lead? Take a deep dive into self-reflection and make sure you know what you want before you give up everything that you have worked so hard for.

Eight of Wands

Daily Incantation: "I accomplish my goals swiftly and gracefully."

Magical Meaning: Charlie has gained complete control of her competitors and immediately sends a powerful fire attack spell toward the other Witchlings. You now have the space to quickly move forward, with a clear path to achieve your maximum potential. The high energy of the Eight of Wands will shoot you ahead, helping you accomplish your goals faster than before. Go with the flow, and let yourself welcome the powerful movement forward. Keep the momentum, and let your drive take you to the finish line.

"Take that, Witchlings!"
—Charlie, Determined Witchling Leading the Contest

Shadow Magic: Shooting off fast like the Eight of Wands may be what you usually do, but sometimes it is wise to slow down and think of your next steps before you take action. There might be a more accessible path to your goal that you haven't noticed before. When you are rushing toward your goal, you do not fully complete the small steps that are needed to get there. There might be important details that you are missing because you just flew by them, ready to accomplish your goals. Instead of allowing you to reach your destination faster, this actually might slow you down. The little tasks that you have bypassed could create more chaos and obstacles later. Hop off that broom, stay in the present, focus on the task in front of you, and take it one step at a time.

Nine of Wands

Daily Incantation: "I am always prepared and ready for good things to come my way."

Magical Meaning: After easily defeating another Witchling contestant in the forest, Charlie can sense that success is within reach. This was a tough battle trail, and she fought hard. It's obvious she is exhausted, but the fire is still burning bright inside of her. Charlie is ready to win it all. You've been in an ongoing battle, fighting through tough times, fighting your hardest and giving it your all. You have endured some hardships, but you know that every time you overcome another challenge, it makes you a stronger Witchling. You have the inner fire to win any battle that you come across. Keep on defending what you've worked so hard for. In the meantime, you will see positive abundance coming your way. You are almost to the finish line! Keep it up.

"Almost to the finish line, George. We can do it!"
—Charlie, Worn-Out Witchling Apprentice

Shadow Magic: Challenge after challenge is blasting into your life, pushing you back with each step you take forward. You are ready to throw down your wand and wave the white flag; you don't know if you can handle these struggles any longer. Just so you know, you are very close to achieving your goal. The reversed Nine of Wands is here to tell you that yes, things have sucked for a long time, but keep going. Think of where you want to be and what you want to have instead of thinking about where you are right now. Dig deep and find the fire burning inside of you. Draw upon your inner strength and face one more battle. Georgie says you've got this!

Ten of Wands

Daily Incantation: "I am excellent at managing my time."
Magical Meaning: Charlie has defeated the last Witchling contestant. She captured all of their wands and is now taking them to the finish line to win the apprenticeship contest. The extra energies from the wands are weighing down on her and making it difficult to move, but she is *so close* to winning. Charlie knows that once she finishes, she can drop the wands and the additional energy overloading her will disappear. You've taken on an

extra workload or burden. This could mean even more responsibility than before, and it weighs you down. Although it's making your life more challenging than ever before, you know that once you are done—once you have finished with this task or project—the heavy weight will be lifted, and you will feel lighter than before. You know that this is only a brief struggle, and you are almost at the finish line.

"And the winner is ..."

–Professor Flores, Witch Superior and Fire Queen of Wands

Shadow Magic: There's a limit to how much pressure one person can handle, even for a short amount of time. Are you trying to do too much at once, all by yourself? Are you shouldering so much weight that you are going to collapse before you reach the finish line? In your desire to help everyone else, your own life has suffered. Give some of that responsibility up; share it with others. You don't have to do it all. Make sure you take care of yourself first. After all, if you burn out, you won't be able to help anyone else.

House of Pentacles

Elemental Magic: Earth

House Protector: Tanuki

Energy: Manifestation

Colors: Banana yellow and brown

Magical Tool: Carved crystal pentacle discs that boost the Witchling's earth magic. These pentacle discs can only be activated by someone with earth magic.

Witchling Personalities: Loves luxury, beauty, nature, and animals. Very materialistic; loves good food and wine. The perfect person to take on a glamping trip! These Apprentices usually graduate to become chefs or caretakers of magical creatures or the land.

Ace of Pentacles

Daily Incantation: "I attract prosperity and abundance."

Magical Meaning: The elemental house protector for the House of Pentacles is the humble and resourceful tanuki. In the House crest, he is standing confidently, like a king, guarding his pentacle. His earth magic infuses patience and grounding energy throughout the House. You have been selected to go on a new adventure. You are about to start on a new path to success. It may be a new job, career, business opportunity, or something else that has to do with material wealth. The Witchlings of the House of Pentacles will tell you that this can be a blessing, but keep in mind that if you want to be powerful in your manifesting, you also have to do the physical work that goes along with it. If you are selected into the House of Pentacles, you will always be loyal to those that deserve your trust. You fight hard and fair to get what you want.

> "Welcome to the House of Pentacles. Eat, drink, and be merry."
> —Aleksandra Zivanovic, Earth Queen to the
> House of Pentacles and Witch Superior

Shadow Magic: If you recently received good news about money or anything to do with finances, like a raise, you might not want to get your hopes up. The Ace of Pentacles showing up reversed could be a sign that the deal will not go through or there may be complications. Please don't spend your money until it is securely in your bank account and all the loose ends have been tied up.

Two of Pentacles

Daily Incantation: "I can easily balance
all my tasks with beauty and grace."

Magical Meaning: Charlie is taking some extra time with George to practice her earth magic. She has to put in more work than the other Witchlings in the House of Pentacles because she is juggling four magical elements instead of just one. You may wish to feel the grounding magic of the Pentacles right now because you are juggling a lot of important things and your life is a bit chaotic, but guess what, Witchling? You can do it! Things aren't as complicated as you're making them out to be. Manage your time, energy, and resources well, and you will not lose your balance. You can handle any challenges that are thrown at you.

> "Mmm, earth magic feels very different from
> fire magic, but still somehow interconnected ..."
> —Charlie, First Year Witchling Training in the House of Pentacles

Shadow Magic: The Two of Pentacles reversed is warning you that you might have overcommitted and are being overwhelmed by your schedule. You might appear put together on the outside, but you are a stressed-out mess. Get your life organized and prioritize what is most important to you. Say no to opportunities that do not align with your path. Do this before everything in your life falls out of balance, including your sanity.

Three of Pentacles

Daily Incantation: "I love collaborating and working with others."

Magical Meaning: Charlie and her friends from the House of Pentacles are gathered in the common room working on a group assignment for class. Everyone in her group has a very different idea of how to approach the task, but interestingly enough, they are all on the same page. Like Charlie, gather up a team of people to support you on your path to success. The Three of Pentacles asks you to collaborate and work with others to achieve your goals. Even if you are the leader, let others speak their mind and see the value they bring. Working with a group can help you manifest your dreams even faster. Remember, there is no "I" in "team."

> "The Witchlings in the of House of Pentacles are so easy to work with."
> –Charlie, First Year Witchling at the Academy

Shadow Magic: Okay, so you have a team to work with, but working with each other is difficult. No one is on the same page, and there is no forward movement on the project. Everyone wants to lead, and the communications between the team is not there. To get realigned with the flow of the project, establish a new structure that works for the team. Be clear on what everyone's views are. New rules need to be laid out in detail before moving on to prevent future misunderstandings.

Four of Pentacles

Daily Incantation: "I love to make money,
spend money, and save money."

Magical Meaning: A few House of Pentacles Witchlings are so stressed out about their schoolwork that their stomachs are aching. Charlie has locked herself in her room and is using her last remaining Pentacles discs to soothe and heal her stomach. When the Four of Pentacles shows up, it is suggesting that you are in preservation mode. You are scared that if you don't save up your money or your energy right now, it might all magically disappear. Don't let this scarcity mindset keep you from enjoying your life. Money and energy work best when they are kept flowing—both in and out. Blocking your energy from going out can also prevent energy from flowing in. Find a flow that you are comfortable with so you can live a fulfilled life while still saving up for the future.

> "I'm using earth magic to heal myself before I help anyone else."
> –Charlie, the Witchling with a Really Bad Stomachache

Shadow Magic: Indulging in all your desires and having a shopping spree might bring you joy at the time, but when the bill comes, you will probably regret it. The Four of Pentacles appears upside down when you are overspending and not being responsible. Remember that those material things will not bring you ultimate happiness. Take a look at your relationship with money before you spend another cent. What does money mean to you? What does real abundance mean to you?

Five of Pentacles

Daily Incantation: "I attract positive opportunities into my life."
Magical Meaning: Even though Charlie and her friend Katie feel like crap, they want to attend a party that is being thrown by one of their housemates.

Unfortunately, no one is letting them in. Unbeknownst to them, the door is unlocked and they could easily enter, if only they explored further. It may seem like no one is there to support you right now. You might feel as if you are being kicked out, ignored, or abandoned. You may have recently reached the lowest of lows and feel like there is no hope. Know that people are nearby to support and help you, but it's up to you to notice that they are there. Take the first step and reach out for help.

> "I feel so alone out here in the cold."
> —Charlie, Year One Witchling, to her Friend Katie

Shadow Magic: The Five of Pentacles in reverse means that there is an end to your challenging times. The loss that you are experiencing will be turned around, and good fortune will soon come your way. It might be from a new job, a unique opportunity, or someone helping you out. Things are starting to look up again.

Six of Pentacles

Daily Incantation: "I give and receive money with ease."

Magical Meaning: Charlie is the first Witchling to be healed of the stomachache that is circling the House of Pentacles. She feels better than before, and her magic is replenished. Charlie decides that she wants to share her healing magic with her fellow Witchlings. You seem to be the most abundant person around, and you are sharing it with others. You've worked so hard to get to where you are; pay it forward through charity. Sharing your wealth and energy brings you joy and fulfillment. Every donation, whether of time or money, is cherished and will come back to you with double the good vibes.

> "Pentacles activate maximum healing strength."
> —Charlie, the Stomach-Bug Healer

Shadow Magic: The reversed Six of Pentacles might indicate that others are taking advantage of you. For instance, you are always helping out your friend, but they do not return the favor. There is no exchange of energy; it only flows one way—from you to them. Either find a way to balance out the transactions or learn to say no.

Seven of Pentacles

Daily Incantation: "I see my investments growing bigger and better every day."

Magical Meaning: Charlie has worked hard all week on her project for the Earth Magical Fair. She didn't have enough time to work on it because of her sickness, but she was able to catch up by staying focused and committed to her studying. The success that you are receiving from your project reflects the hard work and time that you have put into it. You are seeing the big picture and looking toward the future for a long term goal. It is not all about instant gratification for you. You are devoted to the cause, and you're in it for the long run. Keep on going, but make sure that you only work on things that are aligned with your goals. Don't waste your time on tasks that will not help you move forward.

> "Wow, earth magic is so much work, but I love
> studying and strengthening my powers."
> –Charlie, First Year Witchling, to her Parakeet George

Shadow Magic: The shadow side of the Seven of Pentacles reveals that what you are currently investing in is not worth your while. You may be spending money or time on a project that is either not going to benefit you or one that simply won't work out in the long run. If you see that a project is not going to go anywhere, it is time to cut your losses and move on. Focus your time and money on other things that provide value for your life.

Eight of Pentacles

Daily Incantation: "I am a master of my craft."

Magical Meaning: Charlie is practicing hard for her earth magic presentation. For her project, she has decided to use her earth elemental power and Pentacles discs to grow fruit plants and make them flourish. The Eight of Pentacles is about commitment and dedication to what you are doing and mastering your current skill. More projects and exciting career opportunities are presenting themselves as more and more people become aware of your upgraded skill set. These new paths might require more education and studying, but if you avoid distractions and keep practicing the skill, you will undoubtedly master it and gain the success that you desire. Practice makes perfect, but make sure you are practicing the right way.

"Plants grow faster and stronger with loving energy and words of encouragement. That is the secret to my earth magic success."
–Charlie, House of Pentacles Witchling Taking the Earth Magic Exam

Shadow Magic: Don't get too stuck in the Eight of Pentacles energy by trying to be utterly perfect. Your drive to be perfect might be stopping you from adapting to the challenges that are currently hindering your project. Trying to control everything can also prevent you from finding the solutions that you need to move forward. Understand that no one, and nothing, is perfect. You don't need to be perfect to see the beauty in imperfection.

Nine of Pentacles

Daily Incantation: "I attract material wealth and abundance into my life."

Magical Meaning: Charlie's fruit plant project is a successful one, and one of the best in her class, earning her an A+. Her hard work has paid off. George, the rest of the Witchlings, and the professors compliment her as they eat the yummy fruits. Nine of Pentacles suggests that the hard work you've put in will bring abundance into your life. With the security and freedom that material wealth can bring you, you can enjoy the life that you worked hard for. Take time to relax and enjoy the fruits of your labor. You've earned it. Make sure to congratulate yourself on this magnificent achievement.

"Yum, all these fruits look delicious."
–George, the Hungry Parakeet

Shadow Magic: An upside down Nine of Pentacles could mean that you are working your broomsticks off to build your empire. You are so busy with work that you haven't taken any time to enjoy the wealth you are accumulating. Abundance is not all about money; being truly abundant is being able to feel fulfilled and happy in your life. Live your life. Don't miss out on amazing experiences because you are too busy working.

Ten of Pentacles

Daily Incantation: "I am grateful and satisfied with my life."

Magical Meaning: Charlie and her new Pentacles family are gathered in the common room celebrating a successful Earth Magical Fair. Charlie's magical project was an abundant success. Her plant growth magic will be talked about for decades. After a long journey of attaining material wealth (like a successful investment, career, or anything to do with money and recognition), you have finally made a name for yourself. You have completed your goal of gathering abundance for yourself and your loved ones. This success will be remembered for a long time. You, dear Witchling, are a legend.

"I am so grateful that my Pentacles project was a huge success!"
–Charlie, First Year Witchling

Shadow Magic: The shadow side of the Ten of Pentacles is that you lack the drive to attain wealth and abundance. You might be acting lazy, preventing you from achieving your goals, so you are experiencing (or going to experience) a financial loss. Don't focus on the money, but focus on what kind of life you can create with the money that you earn. It doesn't have to be all about the wealth. Being abundant can mean different things to each person. What is your reason for, and definition of, having an abundant life?

House of Cups

Elemental Magic: Water

House Protector: Rainbow Serpent

Energy: Intuition

Colors: Silvery gray and light green

Magical Tool: Cups, which specialize in potions and control water. Cups can help you channel high magic energies for a Water Attack. Create whatever potions you desire just by thinking of the ingredients; they will manifest into the cup.

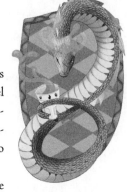

Witchling Personalities: Poets, dreamers, creative artists, and Witchlings who loves to dress up! These apprentices usually graduate to become community healers, inventors, or entertainers.

Ace of Cups

Daily Incantation: "I am abundant in love."

Magical Meaning: You can find the rainbow serpent magically swimming on the House crest. The intuitive, loving, and healing energy of the rainbow serpent is well represented by the Cups. Dive deep into relationships, connections, and feelings with the water magic from this House. Swim into your creative soul and express who you really are. When you let your emotions flow into your actions and work, you will see new opportunities swimming into your life. If you are inspired to pursue a new hobby, start on a new project, or even to get into a new relationship, go for it! If you are confident about who you are and how you honestly feel, you will lead a happy life overflowing with abundance. Follow your heart and allow your imagination to unlock your highest potential. If you are selected into the House of Cups, you know that following your heart is essential to living a joyous life.

Shadow Magic: When the Ace of Cups is flipped upside down, your emotions are blocked. For some reason, maybe even unknown to you, you do not want to express how you feel to the world. You want to keep your emotions locked up tightly inside of you. You might be embarrassed by what you are feeling or fear what will happen if you express yourself. If you are unable to share your feelings right now, that is perfectly fine. You do not need to share everything you feel with others. But you should still get it out of your system. You could take up kickboxing and punch out your frustrations, journal, write a song, or talk it out with your pets.

Two of Cups

Daily Incantation: "I have loving relationships."

Magical Meaning: Charlie thought she might have a hard time finding a friend in this new House, but everyone is as friendly as they say. She finds a partner in crime named Maddie in her first potions class. The Two of Cups represents the mutual love that flows between two people. If this card pops up in your reading, it could mean that you are starting a new loving relationship or renewing your affection for someone in your life. This relationship could be with a lover, business associate, or maybe even a BFF. This relationship will be a good partnership and have mutual benefits, with both of you giving and receiving equally. Being with each other feels natural and magical. You will make some awesome memories together.

Shadow Magic: When the energy and emotions between two people are blocked, it could cause miscommunication in the relationship. The reversed Two of Cups means there are challenges in your relationship. To reclaim your trusting, loving relationship, learn how to communicate with each other with an open mind and heart. Express how you truly feel, and honor both opinions. You have to trust and forgive each other if you want to stay in the relationship.

Three of Cups

Daily Incantation: "I am magnetic, and people love to hang around me."

Magical Meaning: Charlie's new housemates wanted to throw a big welcome party for her. The Three of Cups energy is the ultimate representation of the House of Cups: the power of creativity, fun, celebration, sisterhood, and friendship. Take the time to celebrate your success and happiness with loved ones. Let your family and friends support you and help you reach your highest potential. Have the time of your life! Cheers to new friends and the adventures you will have together.

"Cheers!"
–Charlie, Maddie, and Jen, Witchlings in the House of Cups

Shadow Magic: Celebrating and partying with your loved ones can be fun, but when you overindulge, it can cause you to become unbalanced. Partying is taking over your life, and nothing else seems important. Maybe it is time to cut back from all that partying and face up to reality. Stop numbing yourself with distractions. It's time to put your heart back in the right place.

Four of Cups

Daily Incantation: "I accept new opportunities that bring joy to my heart."

Magical Meaning: Charlie is taking her midterm potions exam, and she doesn't remember the last ingredient of a potion on the exam. Like Charlie, you might be stuck, but don't worry, help and new opportunities will be flowing your way. Some of these ideas or projects might not be for you, so you are turning them down and saying no. It's okay to refuse an opportunity if it doesn't resonate with you or your goals. Decide with your heart. Ask youreslf, "Will saying yes to this new offering bring happiness into my life?" If it doesn't feel right to you, turn it down. Only say yes to things that you are passionate about and things that are aligned with your future goals.

> "This potions exam is driving me insane. What is the
> last magical ingredient that I'm missing?"
> —Charlie, Confused Witchling

Shadow Magic: Right now, you might need a moment to yourself. If you feel like you want to be alone, then follow your heart and take that time for yourself. Don't force yourself to say yes to others to please them. But make sure you don't shut out your loved ones, because sometime in the future when you are ready, you will want to hang out with them again. For now, take some time to meditate, practice Tarot, binge-watch shows, or read a magical book. Love and honor who you are and how you feel currently.

Five of Cups

Daily Incantation: "I release my negative experiences
to the moon with grace and ease."

Magical Meaning: Time is running out during the potions exam, and Charlie is so flustered that she accidentally knocks over and spills one of her cups. The spill costs her precious time, so she is unable to complete her exam and fails one of the most important exams in the class. The Five of Cups tells you that although the situation didn't turn out the way you wanted it to and you might be disappointed in the results, you can't let it hold you back. Don't get stuck on self-pity and lock yourself in a broomstick closet. Witchling, no matter how much that achievement meant to you, it's time to put it in the past and move on.

> "Suck it up, Charlie. Don't cry over spilled potions."
> —George, Charlie's Parakeet Familiar

Shadow Magic: You have been holding onto your failure for way too long. Five of Cups reversed suggests it is time for you to forgive yourself and shower yourself with love. Whatever incident that has occurred is not your fault. Let go of your negative thoughts so you can move forward with an open heart.

Six of Cups

Daily Incantation: "I have a lot of amazing memories that make me happy."
Magical Meaning: Professor Topaz decides to help Charlie out and gives her another chance on the exam. Charlie remembers her kindhearted professor's help and wants to pay it forward. The Six of Cups takes you on a trip to the past, reminiscing about a happy, joyous time and revisiting a loving memory. You might also be making a trip to the past physically by reuniting with old friends and loved ones you haven't seen in a while. These connections from your past are here to remind you of the fun you had. Bring that magic and positive energy to the present so you can allow yourself to be more playful and creative. Connect with your heart's desires.

> "I believe that you can do this, Charlie."
> —Professor Topaz, Charlie's Favorite Professor at this Moment

Shadow Magic: When the Six of Cups shows up reversed in your readings, you are being warned to stop living in the past because you are losing your hold on the present. Don't get stuck on missed opportunities or the good times that have happened. If you keep thinking about the past, you miss out on the amazing things that are trying to flow into your life right now. Let yourself learn from past lessons and move on. Focus on the now. Put your heart and soul into what is going on in the present so that you can create a future you will love.

Seven of Cups

Daily Incantation: "I know what I want, and I attract what is best for me."

Magical Meaning: Potions spells are tricky, and sometimes they can give you the illusion that everything is okay. Then, all of a sudden, boom! Your magical potion explodes. Charlie is studying like crazy so she is prepared to retake her midterm potions exam. The Seven of Cups could mean that you do not have realistic goals. Is it wishful thinking? You keep daydreaming about what will happen in the future, but you are not taking action in the present to help you achieve your goals. This shows that you are not ready to put in the work to fulfill your dreams. Stop spending your time on visualization—it's time to take action and make it happen.

> "It's so booooring watching Charlie visualize, but I guess if
> it's going to help her pass her test, I can endure this."
> —George, the Bored Parakeet Familiar

Shadow Magic: If you have too much Seven of Cups energy in your life, you might be overwhelmed with choices. You don't know what path to take next. It may seem as if these choices are as hard as memorizing potions spells. The easiest thing for you to do is to narrow down your choices, follow your heart, and know that you do not need to be looking for the next big thing. Make a decision and create magic.

Eight of Cups

Daily Incantation: "I am embracing the changes
that are coming my way with beauty and joy."

Magical Meaning: Charlie needs a break. The pressure to pass the potions exam weighs heavily on her. George suggests that she take a break and clear her head. What Charlie is currently doing is not working. It's time to get away for a while. Face it Witchling; your heart is not in it anymore, and there is nothing else to gain from this situation. To move forward, you have to leave behind what is not aligned with your goals, even if it breaks your heart and brings you sadness and disappointment.

"Why don't you get away for a while and come visit me?"
–Aran, Charlie's Handsome Magical Mate

Shadow Magic: If the shadow Eight of Cups is in play, then that means you are ready to try one more time. You've taken your time to listen to what your heart is telling you, and it is time for you to say yes. Before you decide, make sure that what you are doing is bringing joy into your life. Is it aligned with your path?

Nine of Cups

Daily Incantation: "I am grateful for the amazing life that I live!"

Magical Meaning: Nine of Cups is often known as the wish card. It's a sign that your wish is granted. Charlie ends up passing the exam with one of the highest scores in the history of the academy, creating potions of perfection. You've worked hard, and everything that you've been dreaming of is coming true. Your heart is overflowing with joy, and you are loving life. If your wish hasn't come true yet, don't worry—this is a sign that your wish will soon be granted.

"After all that hard work and believing in myself,
my wish came true! That is the formula to success."
—Charlie, Satisfied Witchling Apprentice

Shadow Magic: You will find that not everyone will cheer on your successes and accomplishments. Some already have Corrupt Magic creeping into their heart, and they are full of jealousy and envy. They might try to take you down with them by poisoning you with their negativity. Don't let those people get to you. Instead, keep working toward your goals.

Ten of Cups

Daily Incantation: "I bring all my desires and wishes into reality."
Magical Meaning: There is *another* party in the House of Cups. Everyone is celebrating because the housemates passed their potions exam and are ready to move on to the next level of water magic. Congratulations to you for creating a life of joy and harmony for yourself and your loved ones. You have succeeded, and in doing so, the life of everyone around you has also been elevated. The emotional and physical challenges that you went through to get here have all been worth it. Raise your cup and toast the ones that have supported you along the way.

"Best friends forever, Charlie! Let's party!"
—Maddie, Charlie's House of Cups BFF

Shadow Magic: The reversed Ten of Cups indicates that you are disconnected from your loved ones at this time. You do not feel emotionally fulfilled around them, and your idea of the relationship is different from reality. Check in with your heart and see if this is only temporary. Is it a rough patch that all relationships have to endure to come out stronger? If you've thought it over and concluded that you can't salvage the relationship, then maybe it is time to separate and move on.

House of Swords

Elemental Magic: Air
House Protector: Pegasus
Energy: Intellect
Colors: Sky blue and heather gray

Magical Tool: Swords, which are cunning and strategic in battle. When combined with air magic, Swords Witchlings are fearsome warriors. They are swift, silent, and deadly with their sword. Witchlings with air magic can also create tornados and wind with their swords.

Witchling Personalities: Studious; love to write spells and plan strategies. These Apprentices usually graduate to become bookkeepers, teachers, or the strategists behind battling Corrupt Magic.

Ace of Swords

Daily Incantation: "I am seeing and thinking with a clear, focused mind."

Magical Meaning: The elemental protector for the House of Swords is the striking pegasus. You can find this enchanted, winged creature on the House of Swords crest. The pegasus dashes through the sky with speed and precision, much like the Witchlings of this House during the Swords Duel. A brilliant new idea or breakthrough is swinging through your mind right now. This card could also mean you have suddenly figured out a solution to a challenge that you've been contemplating. Whatever it is, you are finally getting clarity, and your thoughts are falling into place. Have an open mind, and be ready for the new opportunities coming your way. The Witchlings selected into this House are quick-witted and intelligent. They can see through riddles and illusions and have infinite imagination. Everyone at the academy knows this is the House for geniuses.

Shadow Magic: The reversed Ace of Swords can mean that you have so many ideas flying through your mind that you don't know which ones you should pursue. Having too many ideas at once can cause confusion and indecision. Before you start working on a new project, be clear about your intentions and what you want to accomplish so that you can take the most direct path to your goal.

Two of Swords

Daily Incantation: "I know exactly what I want and deserve in my life."

Magical Meaning: Charlie is having a hard time settling into the House of Swords. This House seems to be less social than the other Houses, and Charlie senses hostile energies from some of them. She has to decide if she wants to stay and continue her magical studies at this House or if she'd rather go back to one of the other Houses, where they welcomed her with open arms. The Two of Swords suggests that you are stuck between two choices, much like Charlie. You have to make a difficult decision, and it's hard to choose. Both options seem to be equal in the pros and cons, and you are unsure which path to take. To make sure you select the best possible choice, use your mind and intuition to decide which option is most aligned with your goals.

> "This House is so unfriendly. What am I going to do?"
> —Charlie, the Newest Witchling in the House of Swords

Shadow Magic: The decision that you have to make between these two choices is impossible. Both options seem to lead you on a negative path. You might lack the details and information you need to make the correct choice, or you may be unable to create a third option for yourself. Remove your blindfold to see clearly so that you can make the best decision possible. The answer may be right in front of you.

Three of Swords

Daily Incantation: "I know what it feels like to be loved."

Magical Meaning: Some of the Witchlings at the House of Swords want Charlie gone, so they play a mean prank on her, casting an illusion spell on a sleeping George. The Three of Swords is the ultimate heartbreak or betrayal card. This card may show up if you are experiencing (or will experience) sorrow, grief, and emotional pain. It can feel as if your heart is being physically stabbed, like Charlie felt when she looked at George. Let go of the pain by releasing your emotions. Cry or shout; that will help you heal. Don't let the pain and suffering keep you stuck. Rather, accept your lessons and move forward. In time, your pain and suffering will lessen and will be able to start filling up your mind and heart with happy experiences.

"George! Are you okay, baby bird?"
–Charlie, Heartbroken Witchling Apprentice

Shadow Magic: Flipping the Three of Swords upside down will cause the swords to fall out so that your healing can begin. Only when you release the swords will your heart heal completely. You do not want the pain to be stuck inside forever. Let go of the pain and suffering so that you can welcome love and happiness into your life.

Four of Swords

Daily Incantation: "I am rested, refreshed, and ready for a new day!"

Magical Meaning: Charlie is feeling overwhelmed with the mind games that the House of Swords Witchlings are playing with her, so she decides to stay in for the rest of the day and take a break. The Four of Swords suggests that it is time to rest up and recharge. You have been going through a tough time lately, causing you to worry and feel stressed. Now you can lay down your sword and take a break so that you can regroup. Take a vacation, go on a retreat, or sleep in. Unload your mind and refresh your magic so that you can become refocused for your next challenge.

> "Zzzzzzzz."
> –Charlie, Resting Witchling Apprentice

Shadow Magic: Reversed Four of Swords is warning you that you are almost out of gas. You need to stop right now or you will burn out. Your energy is dangerously low, probably from working long hours, and if you do not take the time to rest, your body will crash. You will not be able to help anyone then.

Five of Swords

Daily Incantation: "I am considerate, caring, and brave."

Magical Meaning: Charlie confronts the Witchlings that pulled the horrible George prank: Lydia and her friends. After a magical battle in the hallway, Charlie wins this round. She knows that the disagreements between them have not ended yet. Like Charlie, you are in a conflict or disagreement with others, which is causing tons of tension and stress. You feel as if everyone is fighting against you. You might be able to win this round, but at what cost to your friendships? Try to work it out and end this battle nicely instead of by force and attack. Learn to speak your truth, but remember to compromise. Solve your situation with your mind, not your emotions.

> "I think they are just jealous of my powers."
> –Charlie, House of Swords Witchling Apprentice

Shadow Magic: Reversed Five of Swords is telling you that the disagreement that you are stuck in is going nowhere. Both parties refuse to agree or listen to each other. The fighting is just wasting your time; it's a lose-lose for both sides. Why not be the bigger Witchling and make amends so that you can move on to more important things?

Six of Swords

Daily Incantation: "I am moving on to new and better experiences!"

Magical Meaning: Academy Witch Mistress McNally is tired of this House of Swords battle. There will be no bullying in her academy. She steps in and asks Charlie if she would like to go to the exclusive Air Tower to train for the Swords Duel without any distractions. She tells Charlie that the best course of action is to leave all of the negativity behind. The Six of Swords is about leaving behind what you don't need, releasing your baggage, and moving forward. It's time to move on to bigger and better things that will bring happiness and comfort into your life. Focus on what you want, not what you are lacking. This move might be something that you decided on or something that was chosen for you, but either way, it is crucial to your personal growth. The uncertainty and sorrow of leaving it all behind will soon be replaced by mental clarity and new energy. All of what you are experiencing during this journey will help you become a better person.

> "Let's leave the fighting and anger behind so you
> can focus on strengthening your air magic."
> –Academy Witch Mistress McNally, a Very Intelligent Witch

Shadow Magic: Stumbling upon a reversed Six of Swords can suggest that you are resistant to the changes that need to happen for you to move forward. This transition is an essential step to reaching your next goal, but you are reluctant to move on because it feels uncomfortable. The most significant changes happen when you are out of your comfort zone, so push on and stretch your limitations. In doing so, you can level up and grow.

Seven of Swords

Daily Incantation: "I am lucky and fortunate in every way!"

Magical Meaning: Lydia, the leader of the mean Witchlings, is very jealous of Charlie's training at the mysterious Air Tower. She creates a training plan and secretly practices in private to ensure a win at the Swords Duel. The Seven of Swords is like the super spy card. There are times when you need to be intelligent, stealthy, and sneaky. This skill set will come in handy when you have a project or mission that you do not want to reveal to the world yet. It's private, and it shouldn't be anyone else's business, as long as it causes no harm. Keep it tucked away until you are ready to show it.

> "These books and weapons will make me even more powerful than Charlie.
> Come on Cuddles, grab those swords and be quiet."
> —Lydia, Charlie's Witchling Rival

Shadow Magic: The reversed Seven of Swords may suggest that you are keeping a secret from others. It is a deep, dark secret that you do not want anyone to know about. Holding on to this secret can cause you stress and guilt. Confessing may feel terrifying to you, but if you do so, the negative thoughts that are swirling in your mind will be released. Make amends with yourself and share your secret with someone who will support you. You will feel great relief if you do, like the weight falling off your shoulders.

Eight of Swords

Daily Incantation: "I allow myself space and time to find my way."

Magical Meaning: Charlie's private training in the Air Tower is no walk in the park. Academy Witch Mistress McNally has put Charlie through a series of intense air magic training. For today's exercise, Charlie is blindfolded and bound in a field of swords, and she has to get out of this maze only using air magic. The Eight of Swords represents you being bound and restricted in your life, especially with the way you are thinking. Your beliefs are limited, and negative thoughts appear in your mind daily. These thoughts are caused by you being unhappy in your job or relationships, or you might just be feeling unfulfilled in general. You do not see a solution to your challenges. Call upon your inner magic and blast the thoughts that no longer serve you. When you change your mindset, you will start to change your reality. If you substitute negative thoughts with positive ones, your blindfold will fall off.

> "This is the hardest task yet. What if I can't do this?
> What if I'm stuck in this sword maze forever?"
> –Charlie, Frustrated Witchling

Shadow Magic: The Eight of Swords reversed may represent that you are suffering from your own inner critic. You have a habit of putting yourself down and thinking negative thoughts about what you are doing. When you try to accomplish a goal, all you can think about is why you don't deserve it or how you are not good enough, and that leads to failure. Catch yourself when your inner critic shows up, and instead of judging yourself, set a positive intention to succeed.

Nine of Swords

Daily Incantation: "I have soothing dreams, and I always get a good night's sleep."

Magical Meaning: Charlie is tossing and turning tonight, unable to sleep. It could be that she is worried about the Swords Duel that is happening tomorrow, but it feels like more than that. Charlie jolts awake from a disturbing nightmare where she was stabbed. The Nine of Swords suggests that worry, fear, anxiety, or stress is keeping you awake at night. Negative thoughts weigh heavily in your mind, and you can't stop thinking about them. Obsessing over how bad the situation is can only make it worse. You might end up manifesting your nightmares into reality. Instead of constantly worrying about how wrong everything is, replace your worry with positive thoughts and focus on how you will accomplish your goals.

"That nightmare seemed so real..."
–Charlie, Year One Witchling Apprentice

Shadow Magic: When Nine of Swords is upside down, all your fears and worry will be brought out of the shadows and into the light. Instead of dreaming about them, they will become a reality. This is beneficial because now you can take action and solve the situation. Don't be scared of the shadows coming out. Face them head-on and figure out the smartest way to defeat them without hurting yourself or others.

Ten of Swords

Daily Incantation: "I allow positive opportunities to come into my life."
Magical Meaning: Charlie beats Lydia and wins the Swords Duel event. An unhappy Lydia and her mean Witchlings send ten swords into Charlie's back, and she crumples to the ground. Although Charlie is hurt, she is strong. With magic, care, and love from Georgie, she will be better in no time. The Ten of Swords represents a painful ending. It could be getting fired from your job, breaking up with your lover, or a situation that ends abruptly. You never expected this to happen, but it's happening, and you feel betrayed and at a loss. The bright side of this situation is that it's finally over, and you can now move on. You've bottomed out, and there is nowhere else to go but up. The pain and wounds will eventually heal, so learn from this crisis, and move on.

"Bring me a healer right now. It's not too late—we can still save Charlie!"
—Professor Okamoto, Swords Exam Judge

Shadow Magic: You are on the verge of a significant change, but you are fighting it. The ending and change sound scary, and you don't think you are ready for it. If you keep resisting, your misery will continue, and you will not be able to grow. Let go of what is holding you back, even if it's painful, so that you can welcome new opportunities and magic into your life.

The court cards are the characters and rulers of each suit, or in this case, the elemental Houses. They are the Pages, Knights, Queens, and Kings of each House. Court cards can represent a specific person, personalities, yourself, or a situation. The best way to work with court cards is to set an intention before your reading. Decide what energy you will be asking them to show up as.

Pages

Meet the Pages of the Witchling Academy. They are the magical animal familiars to the Witch Superior Queens of each elemental House. They help the Queens keep an eye on the Witchling Apprentices. Pages are the youngest of the court cards, with childlike, curious energy.

Page of Wands

Daily Incantation: "I am grateful to live an exciting and adventurous life."

Magical Meaning: Purrdey, the familiar cat to Professor Flores, is a feisty little guy. He is always looking for a new adventure in the House of Wands, following a different Witchling every moment! The Page of Wands wants you to start a new and exciting experience. Learn about an interest or hobby that makes you happy. Purrdey suggests that you find something that fires you up and chase after it. Pounce on that exciting idea, and explore your inner passions. They say curiosity killed the cat, so we wonder how many lives Purrdey has left? You might not know where you are headed, but if you follow the path that lights you up, you can't go wrong.

Shadow Magic: When too much Page of Wands energy enters your life, you might see this card show up reversed. You are feeling impatient and don't want to commit to anything. For example, you love to start on projects, but you have a hard time finishing them because they don't seem to work out. Not everything will work out on the first try. Be patient and go back to your original concept. Make sure the actions you are taking are aligned with your goals.

Page of Pentacles

Daily Incantation: "I love to eat nourishing and healthy foods that make me feel great."

Magical Meaning: Jinxy, the bunny familiar to Professor Zivanovic, loves to play outside in the vegetable gardens. He helps the House of Pentacles Witchlings keep the garden abundant and organized with fruits and veggies. The Page of Pentacles can be a sign of new beginnings to a creative project that will bring in opportunities regarding money, wealth, material possessions, or physical health. You are beginning to manifest your dreams into reality. Make a plan and hop to it, as this will lead you to your goal. Plant the seed and start planning your manifestation garden.

"Carrots, cabbage, strawberries–I got them all. Come and have a feast with me!"
–Jinxy, Bunny Familiar to Professor Zivanovic, Earth Queen to the House of Pentacles

Shadow Magic: An upside down Page of Pentacles can mean that you are so busy daydreaming about new ideas that you're ignoring the ones that are already there. You have many goals, and it's hard to keep track of what you are doing. Jump on back to the beginning. Why did you want your original goal in the first place? Recommit to your goal and take action to reach your dreams.

Page of Cups

Daily Incantation: "I am full of imagination and creativity."

Magical Meaning: Scullywag, the cutest ferret familiar in the world, belonging to Professor Higuchi, loves to cuddle with everyone. His favorite pastime is playing in the sink and inventing pirate stories with happy endings. The Page of Cups invites you to embrace the new and creative ideas that are splashing into your life. Daydream and stay curious like Scullywag. Just make sure you follow this creative trail and take action, even if it seems out of your reach. Anything is possible if you put your heart into it.

"Ahoy Witchlings, cuddle with me and pet me to sleep please."

–Scullywag, Ferret Familiar to Professor Higuchi, Water Queen to the House of Cups

Shadow Magic: Don't be an extreme Page of Cups and get trapped in your daydreams and imagination. Scullywag knows that your made-up world might be way better than your reality right now, but things will only get worse if you don't wake up and start taking action in real life. You might start seeing your dreams come true.

Page of Swords

Daily Incantation: "I am smart and capable of learning new things with ease."

Magical Meaning: Caydence is the gorgeous owl familiar to Professor Okamoto. She watches over the House of Swords and reports everything back to her mistress with incredible speed. Caydence will often hang around the Witchlings while they study so that she can learn new things. The Page of Swords may soar into your life if you are exploring a new way of thinking or a new idea. Just like Caydence, you hunger for knowledge, and you love it when you have something new to study. The beginning is always exciting, but remember to follow through. Let your enthusiasm for the idea take you to the finish line.

> "Hey little Apprentice, please turn the page for me so
> I can finish reading your interesting book."
> —Caydence, Owl Familiar to Professor Okamoto, Air Queen to the House of Swords

Shadow Magic: The reversed Page of Swords can mean that you are taking action without thinking things through or having a solid plan. You are full of energy, but it's not being used efficiently. Instead of just dive-bombing into situations, make sure you take it step-by-step and examine the conditions first. This will lead you to exciting adventures that are aligned with your life goals.

Knights

Make way for the Knights of the Witching Academy of Magic. These are the guardians of the hallways—hall monitors—and they are who the younger students look up to. They are given extra responsibilities, like facilitating Year One's orientation and monitoring curfew. You can identify the Knights of the academy by the K on their House badges. Knights bring a teenage energy to the card.

Knight of Wands

Daily Incantation: "I am courageous, and I love adventures."
Magical Meaning: Jaymi, a Year Three Witchling, has been a Knight for two years, and she was the youngest to be knighted in the history of the academy. She is courageous and will charge into a fight with no questions asked! The Knight of Wands is hollering at you to be bold and pursue your dreams. If a creative idea has shown up in your life, it is time to chase after it. Be clear about what exactly you want, and your enthusiasm, passion, and motivation will take care of the rest. This inspiring card is giving you the green light to go for it. Just don't get caught after curfew in the hallways

by Knight Jaymi, because she will chase you with Trace, her tiger familiar, until she finds you—she always accomplishes her goals.

> "Let's start a magical fight club! Come at me Witchling!"
> –Knight Jaymi, Year Three Witchling in the House of Wands

Shadow Magic: Knight of Wands reversed can mean that you aren't thinking of the consequences before taking action, and it will get you into lots of trouble. Most times it is advisable to keep your compulsive and destructive behaviors to a minimum. Learn to stop and weigh the pros and cons before you charge in.

Knight of Pentacles

Daily Incantation: "I am reliable and efficient at everything I do."

Magical Meaning: Joanne, a Year Four Witchling, is in charge of the Knights. She monitors the activities and tasks of each Knight and thinks of new and creative ways for them to enforce academy rules. Even though she patrols the hallways with her panda familiar, Jojo, what she loves most is sitting in her Knights tower, organizing and planning away. The Knight of Pentacles suggests that you are very productive and are incredibly set on turning your goals into reality. Keep staying focused and taking the action that you need in order to get one step closer to your goal. Your manifestation garden is starting to sprout. Slow and steady is a good pace, so stick to your plan, and you will eventually accomplish your goals.

> "Okay Knights, this is what we have planned for this week,
> so follow the schedules and things will go smoothly."
> –Knight Joanne, Year Four Witchling in the House of Pentacles

Shadow Magic: Upside down, the Knight of Pentacles warns you not to become obsessed with your achievements. Don't be too focused on working toward one goal because you might be sacrificing everything around you. You don't have to be perfect. Know that who you are and where you are right now is where you are supposed to be. You have enough time in the world to do anything you want; learn to slow down and smell the roses.

Knight of Cups

Daily Incantation: "I am beautiful, charming, and intelligent."

Magical Meaning: This Year Four Witchling, Jessica, is the event coordinator for the academy. Being in charge of all the social gatherings and parties to help the Witchlings bond is her dream job. The Knight of Cups is telling you to follow your dreams. Do you have heart-centered ideas that you want to make come true? Maybe a new hobby is calling to you. Go forth and bring this desire into existence; the only way to do so is if you take physical action. Let your creative ideas flow out of your heart and into real life. If you don't move toward your dream, then that's all it is: a dream. You can find Jessica and her flying fish familiar, Sage, in the hallway, making sure that everyone is having a good time.

 "Let me tell you about the three new Wizards that have a crush on me ..."
–Knight Jessica, Year Four Witchling in the House of Cups

Shadow Magic: When the reversed Knight of Cups shows up in your readings, it might be a sign that you are sharing too much of your energy and time with others. Maybe you need to be a bit selfish and take care of yourself first. You love to bring people happiness and joy, which is a great thing. Just remember that in order for you to show up as your best self, you have to feel like your own cup is full. Start to set some boundaries in a relationship, and don't let others take advantage of you. Know that no one can make you happy except yourself.

Knight of Swords

Daily Incantation: "I can achieve anything I put my mind and magic to."

Magical Meaning: Knight Lexi, Year Four, is at the top of her class. Not only is she gorgeous, but she is one of the most intelligent Witchlings in the academy, managing anything to do with computers and software. The energy of the Knight of Swords is all about taking swift action. Lexi does not wait for things to happen; she takes the initiative and creates momentum for herself to reach her goals. Right now, it is time for you to charge forward and create the action that you need to succeed. You know precisely what you need to do and how to do it, so trust your intellect and the energy of the Knight of Swords to guide you. If you need some help, Lexi's twin Samoyed familiars, Kado and Nola, can help you out.

> "When you are fully activated in all areas of your life and rise to your highest potential, that is when you are the most abundant."
> —Knight Lexi, Year Four Witchling in the House of Swords

Shadow Magic: The reversed Knight of Swords suggests that your thoughts are scattered and all over the place. This can cause you to make impulsive decisions or, even worse, to be indecisive. Before you confuse yourself or the people around you, sort out your mind. Let go of any distractions, and focus on one thing at a time. Choose a goal, and see it to the end before you move on. It will require mental strength to see this through. Do you have it in you?

Queens

A Queen of the House is always a Witch Superior, the highest level of achievement for Witches, with the same elemental power as the House. She is responsible for one of the four Houses in the academy, sort of like a dorm mother. She is there to help the Witchling Apprentices navigate academy life and their magic with ease, but she also lays down the law if needed. The energies of these cards are mature, nurturing, older females.

Queen of Wands

Daily Incantation: "I am full of joy and happiness."

Magical Meaning: Professor Flores is one of the most adored professors at the academy. She loves to blast music in class while the Witchlings work to show them how to have a good time while studying. The Queen of Wands suggests that there is so much you can offer to the world, that there is no room to doubt yourself. Professor Flores encourages her students to come to her with any challenges or issues that they have in the academy. Her motto is "Stay true to your exciting ideas, and be aware of the actions that you are taking." You are an expert at manifesting what you want, and you know how to share your thoughts with others. Believe in the magical fire that you possess, and you can accomplish any goal with ease.

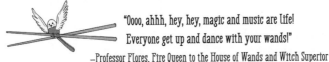

"Oooo, ahhh, hey, hey, magic and music are life!
Everyone get up and dance with your wands!"
–Professor Flores, Fire Queen to the House of Wands and Witch Superior

Shadow Magic: When the Queen of Wands is in shadow, it could be because a mature person that has female energy is showing up in your life. They may be demanding and overbearing. Even though you have said no, this person is very persistent; your refusal has no effect on them. You could also be pushing yourself so hard that you burn out. You've taken on too much. Don't let the Queen of Wands keep you in the shadows—go out and ask for help.

Queen of Pentacles

Daily Incantation: "I am a powerful manifestor."

Magical Meaning: Professor Zivanovic is not only a powerful Witch, she is also the Crown Princess of Senbria. At the House of Pentacles, she teaches the Witchlings how to cook delicious food by growing and gathering it from their very own magical garden. The Queen of Pentacles shows that your manifestation garden is lush and abundant. You have taken time to nurture your garden, and it is ripe for harvest. This Queen card represents the prosperity and security that you have earned as a result of your hard work. The good fortune that you have built can now sustain you and those that you love. Continue to nurture your resources and grow your abundance.

> "Jinxy, let's go relax in the garden, maybe even have a piece of
> chocolate or two, while I look through some paperwork."
> —Professor Zivanovic, Earth Queen to the House of
> Pentacles, Witch Superior, and Princess of Senbria

Shadow Magic: Your poor manifestation garden is withering and dying because of your neglect. The nurturing work you were supposed to do was not done, so there is nothing to harvest. All is not lost; go back to the seeds that you originally planted and revisit those ideas. Think of another way to achieve the goal that would be easier for you to care for. Make sure that this time, you are happy to take action and see your idea grow.

Queen of Cups

Daily Incantation: "I have strong intuitive and psychic abilities."

Magical Meaning: The intuitive Professor Higuchi is always on the move, flowing from one thing to another. You can mostly find her in the classroom with teacups, coffee mugs, and water glasses all around. Professor Higuchi has the biggest heart in the academy, and she truly loves and sees the best in everyone. Not only does she teach water magic to her Apprentices, but she also helps her Witchlings find their path to love and joy daily. The Queen of Cups suggests that you are very creative and intuitive. You are healing to those around you. If there is a challenge that you have to navigate through, follow your instincts and emotions. Read the energies of the situation, and let your inner magic guide you in making the right decisions. Trust your heart and intuition; this will lead you to success.

> "Scully, what do you think of this painting so far?"
> —Professor Higuchi, Water Queen to the House of Cups and Witch Superior

Shadow Magic: You may be so sensitive and in tune with other people's emotions that you drown in them. This causes you to continually feel drained by other people's stories, experiencing them emotionally as your own. You need to learn how to disconnect from other people's drama, even if they are your loved ones. You do not need to hold their fear or pain; that is not your responsibility. Listen to the stories, but do not hold on to them. Take a deep breath and let what is not needed flow out of you.

Queen of Swords

Daily Incantation: "I speak my truth."

Magical Meaning: Nobody can beat Professor Okamoto in a sword duel. She is definitely the Queen of Swords. All the Witchlings look up to her, but they are also a bit scared of her fierceness. Her swords class is no nonsense because she is one of the toughest teachers, but if you listen, you will come out a great Swords Witchling. Right now it is time to be upfront and truthful like Professor Okamoto. There is no time for you to beat around the bush, so don't bother lying. Use your intellect and intuition to communicate effectively, and others will respect your opinions. When you are honest and get straight to the point, it will lessen confusion and you will be able to accomplish your goals faster. Stand tall and be heard.

> "Witchlings, no drama in this class. Leave your problems at
> the door, work hard, and we will get along just fine."
> —Professor Okamoto, Air Queen to the House of Swords and Witch Superior

Shadow Magic: Sometimes being truthful can also be hurtful. You may come across as uncaring or coldhearted because others view you as unemotional. Be aware of how you communicate with others, and be mindful of how it will make them feel. There is a way to share your opinions while still being compassionate. Think of a way to find the balance between these two things so that you do not come off as a mean person to your loved ones.

Kings

The elemental goddesses are the Kings and rulers of the Houses. They aren't out and about in the world much anymore, but they do sometimes hang out with higher-status Wizards and Witches at ceremonies or events. You can pray and call upon them for guidance if needed. These elemental goddesses rule and guard the elemental magic for each House. They are where the magical community gets their powers. The energies of the Kings are masculine, wise, and mature.

King of Wands

Daily Incantation: "I am charming and charismatic; everyone loves me."
Magical Meaning: The fire elemental goddess once raged her fires across the Universe, wanting to conquer it all, but throughout the centuries, she has calmed down. Now she is content with watching over her realm, inspiring and motivating Apprentices in the House of Wands. The King of Wands card says that you've reached a masterful level of manifesting, and it's time to expand your magic in impossible ways. You are in control of what you desire. Know that the outcome of this situation will be up to you, and you will choose how it turns out. If you commit and believe that you will succeed, then you will. You are a powerful manifestor, so be aware of what your thoughts and desires are on a daily basis. If you need additional help, seek the fire goddess when you want to manifest your dreams into

reality...if you can find her. This powerful goddess can't sit still, and she likes to be in on the action.

> "Follow the path of fire and follow me to greatness;
> you will lack nothing if you have passion for your craft."
> –Fire Elemental Goddess, Ruler of Fire Magic and the House of Wands

Shadow Magic: A reversed King of Wands can suggest that the goal that you are setting for yourself right now may be too aggressive. Although it is great to have big dreams, make sure your goals are in your realm of reality. Achieving this goal is up to you. If you believe it, you can achieve it. The challenge with this particular goal is that you don't think that you can reach it; you've set your goal so high that it seems unattainable at this moment in time. Keep this big goal in mind, but for now, set some smaller goals that can help you achieve the big one eventually.

King of Pentacles

Daily Incantation: "I am wealthy, prosperous, and abundant in all areas of my life."

Magical Meaning: The earth elemental goddess, the ruler of earth magic and the House of Pentacles, is all about material wealth and the beautiful things in life. The earth goddess teaches the concept of working together to cultivate wealth. Work smarter, not harder. The King of Pentacles suggests that you are an epic entrepreneur. You know how to start and run a business with abundant success. When you have a vision, you can create an unstoppable plan and gather the best resources to help turn your dreams into reality. You are the goddess of your kingdom, and money flows smoothly into your life. Now that you are at the top of your game, you can help others learn how to be abundant, which will return to you. If you have issues with money and abundance, this is the goddess to call on. She will help you gain riches, but you must be truthful and show her you will be responsible with your money. The earth goddess is a very generous, patient goddess that shares her riches and love with Humdrums and magical beings alike.

"Look at my jewels sparkling in the sun.
No one is richer or more abundant than I!"
–Earth Elemental Goddess, Ruler of Earth Magic and the House of Pentacles

Shadow Magic: The reversed King of Pentacles can mean that there is an unhealthy obsession with money, either within you or someone around you. This person loves money so much that they will do whatever it takes to be abundant. They don't care who suffers or is hurt in the process as long as they turn a profit and get everything that they want. If this is you, take a step back and ask yourself if you are willing to sacrifice everything for money. If this is someone around you, it might be wise to let them go so that you don't get hurt as they claw their way to the top.

King of Cups

Daily Incantation: "I am in control of my emotions."

Magical Meaning: The water elemental goddess is one of the most approachable goddesses. She is very even-tempered and in control of her emotions. Leading and bringing people together makes her feel happy and joyous. The King of Cups assures you that when a stressful situation arises, you have the emotional maturity to navigate through the challenge. You are the goddess of your own emotions. Acknowledge all that you are feeling and hold space for yourself. Accept how you feel and let the drama flow out of you as you stay focused on your goal. If you are calling upon this goddess, make sure you have a good bottle of bubbly and a couple of glasses available, because she sure does love a good drink.

"Cheers to a beautiful day, a day of joyful celebrations."
–Water Elemental Goddess, Ruler of Water Magic and the House of Cups

Shadow Magic: The reversed King of Cups is warning you that you may be taking on too much negativity from the people you are taking care of, losing yourself in the process. You are suppressing your own emotions and your well-being for them. If this self-destructive path continues, you will have nothing left for yourself or others. Create firm boundaries and take care of yourself first.

King of Swords

Daily Incantation: "I have all the wisdom and knowledge that I need to solve my challenges."

Magical Meaning: The air elemental goddess is the ruler of everything concerning intellect and the mind. She contains information and wisdom gathered from the past, present, and future. The air goddess holds the magic for communication and mental stimulation. She is an excellent war strategist and has led the kingdom to victory against Corrupt Magic many times, probably because she is a hundred steps ahead of everyone. When making a decision, you need to lead with logic and knowledge instead of emotion. Take time to research the situation with mental clarity. If others are involved in this decision, make sure you stay fair and emotionally detached. If you call on this goddess, make sure you are clear and truthful with your intentions, and she will swiftly help you achieve your goals.

> "Speak the truth from your heart and soul, and I will grant you your wish."
> —Air Elemental Goddess, Ruler of Air Magic and the House of Swords

Shadow Magic: If the reversed King of Swords shows up in your reading, it suggests that there might be an abuse of power. You might be in control or have a lot of authority right now, but you are misusing the power. Are you using your intellect to manipulate others into doing the things you want them to? Please don't take advantage of others because you think you are smarter than them. Instead, use your intellect to help others.

Witchlings, please take your seats. This is your extra credit spells class. It is not required for your initiation, but it will provide awesome tools for you to have in your arsenal. In this class you will learn how to craft your own spell, and at the end, there will be a bonus wishing spell crafted for you.

Working your own crafted spell can be doubly powerful because you personally connect with the energy of the spell. The main structure for spell-crafting will be provided below, and it is up to you if you'd like to add anything extra to it.

How to Craft Your Own Spell

1. It is important to set an intention before starting your spell. Make sure that your intention is really specific, full of details. This is true for all spells.

2. Select magical tools like Tarot, candles, crystals, and essential oils that relate to your intention. Make sure the tools you select energetically match with your intentions. For example, you can select the Nine of Pentacles, a green candle, cinnamon oil, and citrine for abundance and wealth. Do research and experiment to find out what tools work best together.

3. You don't need to write words for an actual spell, but it does help connect the spiritual plane to the physical plane, so it is always encouraged. And no, it does not have to rhyme!

4. For best results, visualize the intention coming true. You can visualize the outcome while you are holding your crystal, staring at the

Tarot card, lighting a candle, or inhaling essential oil. Whatever you choose will be right. Let your intuition guide you.

5. Always end the spell or ritual with thanks, either to the Universe or whomever you believe in. If you are working with the energies of the moon, make sure you thank her.

Witchling Warning: Undiluted essential oils should never be applied directly to your skin. Make sure to add a base or carrier oil, like coconut oil, to your essential oils if you choose to apply them to your skin. Some oils are not meant to be applied to the skin at all, so make sure to read about your oil before use. The best way to use essential oils is to diffuse your oils in a water-based diffuser. The diffuser will disperse a vapor into the air so that it can be safely absorbed by your body.

There is no right or wrong way to craft a spell. Make sure you take notes so you can see what works for you and what doesn't. Remember, the simpler the better. What you do is totally up to you, and it should be whatever feels right to you, using whatever tools you have available.

Remember: Spells do not guarantee 100 percent success! Wish for what you believe you can receive. If you think manifesting a billon dollars is out of your reach, it will not come true. Also, you can't just wait for things to happen. You have to put in some effort and take physical action.

"Spells are mostly about your energy and intention."
–Charlie, Year One Witchling Apprentice

Wishing Spell: This is a general wishing spell that anyone can do. Use this spell to manifest your life, asking for the highest good and the outcome that is best for you.

Magical Tools:
   Nine of Cups card
   Pen or pencil
   Paper
   Smoky quartz crystal
   Lemon essential oil mixed with a carrier oil (or a fresh lemon peel)

1. Gather all your tools and set them in front of you. Make sure you are in your sacred space, where no one will bother you during your spell work. Cleanse the space of negative energy; sage if you wish.

2. Drop one drop of the premixed lemon essential oil onto your palm. Rub your palms together. Put your palms by your nose and inhale and exhale three times. As you inhale, breathe in clarity and focus. As you exhale, release all your stress and confusion.

3. Now pick up your smoky quartz and hold it in your hands. Imagine your wish and intention coming true, as if it has already happened. Visualize how happy you are. Who is around you celebrating? What are you hearing? What you are tasting in this visualization? Be as detailed as possible. When you are finished, put your crystal down.

4. Next, focus on the Nine of Cups and ask if there is a message for you to help you reach your goals. Write down whatever pops into your mind, anything at all. If you don't get anything, just write down how you feel after achieving your goals. What does the Nine of Cups mean to you in this spell, and what is your card telling you?

5. When you are finished, thank the Universe. Expect your wish to manifest, but don't forget to take physical action to make it happen!

6. Keep the Nine of Cups and your crystal someplace special or close by, like on your altar or next to your bed, for nine days. Whether

your intentions have already manifested or you are still waiting, thank your crystal and card on the ninth day. Sending out gratitude will amplify your wish and attract positive opportunities. After giving thanks, you may put the card back into the deck. As for your crystal, cleanse it and use the stone for another spell or continue to keep it near you for good vibes.

Welcome, Witchling Apprentice, to your final exams! For these final exams, you will be performing Tarot spreads using your knowledge of the Tarot cards, intuition, and inner magic by applying the lessons you have learned at the Witchling Academy of Magic.

Tarot spreads are cards laid out in a specific pattern. Each position in the layout has a unique energy and meaning, but all positions are related to the ultimate question of the reading. The spread adds a deeper layer of understanding to your questions and challenges. There are tons of spreads out there, but for your exams, you will just be working with these three that were magically created for you. All you have to do is follow the instructions in each spread and lay out your cards.

For Year One newbies, it's okay if you don't fully understand what is going on. The more you work with Tarot, the more you practice and keep pulling cards and doing spreads, the more you will understand. One day, it will just "click" for you!

Magical Message from Academy Witch Mistress McNally: Dear Witchling, look how far you've come this year in the academy! All the professors and I are so proud of your dedication. There are no right or wrongs, and everyone who attempts a spread will pass their finals! So what are you waiting for? Here is a magical tip for you: after you lay out the cards, read them with your intuition first. See what jumps out at you and how the cards make you feel, then check for additional meanings in this handbook. Afterward, read all your cards together like a story. See you at the initiation ceremony!

Basic Three-Card Spread: This spread is great for Year One Apprentices and newbies who haven't really worked with Tarot. It is easy to read, to the point, and one of the most popular spreads out there. There are alternative meanings that you can switch out for each position, but let's just stick to this one for our exam.

- Position 1: Past, what has already happened, what got you to where you are now.
- Position 2: Present, what is happening right now, what energy is around you at this moment.
- Position 3: Future, what will happen if you follow this path, what will show up in the future.

Activate My Witchling Magic Spread: Everyone has magic. Even Humdrums have a bit of magic, they just choose not to recognize it because that feels safer. You—especially you—are full of magic, and this spread will help you discover how to awaken your inner magic so you can shine inside and out! The secret to claiming your magic is to be aware and acknowledge it.

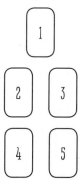

- Position 1: What is the magical essence of my true self?
- Position 2: How do others see me?
- Position 3: How do I see myself?
- Position 4: What is my inner magic?
- Position 5: What actions can I take to activate my magic and be my true self?

Magical Broom Spread: Do you have doubts, blocks, or challenges that you can't seem to sweep away? This spread will help you figure out exactly what is blocking you from reaching your goals. It will sweep out any negative energies that you don't need anymore so you can make room for positive opportunities to come your way.

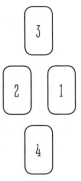

- Position 1: What negative dust bunny is blocking me from moving forward?
- Position 2: How can I sweep away this blockage so I can move on with my life?
- Position 3: What sparkling new opportunity is waiting for me to claim?
- Position 4: What actions can I take to claim my new opportunity?

Initiation Ceremony

Dear Witchling Apprentice,

Cue the confetti ...

Congratulations on your initiation into the Witchling Academy! This was an exciting and fantastic year for all of us at the academy, with so many talented students attending. We hope you take everything that you have learned at the academy and apply it to your everyday life. Remember, magic and Tarot are a lifestyle, so infuse them into your daily routines and keep practicing. Never stop learning about both—there will always be more to learn and play with!

Now that you have strengthened your Tarot skills, there are a few options for you. You can read Tarot for yourself, using Tarot privately to further your spiritual journey and overcome your challenges, or you can also share your magic with family and friends and show off this must-have magical tool. Practice and do readings on yourself or others. When you have enough practice and experience in slinging cards, you can start your own Tarot business and read professionally for others (if you so choose). Whatever you decide to do with your Tarot magic, make sure it feels good to you and that you are happy doing it.

Have a witchy summer break, and we welcome you back next year for another magical adventure at the Witchling Academy of Magic.

Sincerely,
Maria McNally
Academy Witch Mistress

Witches, Wizards, and Magical Beings

Air Elemental Goddess: The air elemental goddess is the King of Swords. Legend says that she invented the first sword that channeled air magic. She rules over the House of Swords and, on rare occasions, you might see her floating around the library with her butterflies. The elemental power of air was her gift to the realm.

Aran Goundar: Aran is a Wizard Apprentice and Charlie's magical mate and boyfriend. They instantly had a connection during their fated meeting at the All Hallows' Eve Ball, which you can see in The Lovers card. He is handsome, adventurous, and funny. Aran possess the elemental magic of fire. His magical familiar is Silverback, a serious, gray-and-white wolf.

Ashlyn Ward: Ashlyn, also known as Ash, is in the House of Wands. She is one of Charlie's BFFs. Ash's elemental power is fire. She has long, peachy-orange hair. Her magical familiar is Moonbite, a white owl.

Charlotte "Charlie" Lee: Charlie is the hero of this story. She is the only Witchling in the history of the Light Realm that possesses all four elemental magics. She is the only Witchling Apprentice to ever be placed into all four Houses: the House of Wands, House of Cups, House of Pentacles, and House of Swords. Charlie's biological mother is Christina McNally, the Shadow Witch. Her magical familiar is George, nicknamed Georgie, a baby-blue parakeet.

Earth Elemental Goddess: The earth elemental goddess is the King of Pentacles. She knows how to run a prosperous kingdom and how to keep resources flowing. She is dedicated to helping the Witchlings from the House of Pentacles learn how to work smarter, not harder. She also teaches the Witchlings how to have an abundant flow of prosperity. The elemental power of earth was her gift to the realm.

Emperor Jeff: A handsome, powerful Wizard who commands the elemental magic of fire, Emperor Jeff is the magical mate to Empress Sophia. He is charming and a big flirt, but he is married and completely devoted to his Empress. He is one of the two ruling figures of the Magical Council. His magical familiar is Benson, a ram.

Empress Sophia: The wife and magical mate of Emperor Jeff, Empress Sophia is currently the most powerful and highest-ranking Witch Superior. She believed that Charlie was the unnamed person mentioned in the prophecies about defeating the Shadow Witch. She is one of the two ruling figures of the Magical Council. Her magical familiar is Leira, a white stag.

Fire Elemental Goddess: The fire elemental goddess is the King of Wands. She once ran wild with her magic, igniting the Light Realm with fire. Over the centuries, she has calmed down. Now she is passionate about motivating the Witchling Apprentices in the House of Wands. The elemental power of fire was her gift to the realm.

Jaymi Elford: Jaymi is a Year Three Witchling Apprentice that has been a Knight for two years. She proudly represents the House of Wands. She loves a good adventure, but she gives out the most detentions at the academy. Her magical familiar is Trace the tiger.

Jessica T. Beckham Jr.: Jessica is the social butterfly of the Knights. She is a Year Four at the academy and was selected into the House of Cups. She has natural charisma and is in charge of all social gatherings for the Witchling Apprentices. Her magical familiar is Sage the flying fish.

Joanne Chow: Joanne is a Year Four Knight Witchling from the House of Pentacles. She is in charge of the Knights, making sure that everything is in order. Organizing is her favorite thing to do; she loves being productive. Jojo the panda is her magical familiar.

Lydia Park: Lydia is a Year One Witchling Apprentice from the House of Swords. She is jealous of Charlie. Lydia and her mean Witchling friends pranked Charlie in the Three of Swords. She also makes an appearance in the Five of Swords, Seven of Swords, and Ten of Swords. Lydia's magical familiar is Cuddles the cheetah.

Madison Bright: Madison, also known as Maddie, is Charlie's BFF from the House of Cups. She is known for her short, mint-green hair. Her magical familiar is Boots, a black cat.

Maria McNally: Acting as the current Academy Witch Mistress of the Witchling Academy of Magic, she is our High Priestess. Academy Witch Mistress McNally is a high-ranking Witch Superior and possesses the elemental magic of air. She is the twin to Christina McNally, the Shadow Witch, which makes her Charlie's auntie. During Maria's schooling at the academy, her elemental magic was ranked number one for all four years. Christina was jealous of all of the attention Maria got from the students and professors, so she searched for ways to gain more power, which was the catalyst that created the Shadow Witch. Her magical familiar is Hex, a calico cat.

Professor Aja Okamoto: A Witch Superior and the Queen of Swords, Professor Okamoto watches over the Witchling Apprentices in the House of Swords. She is the swiftest, most powerful, and most graceful air Witch in the realm. Her magical familiar is Caydence, the orange and yellow owl.

Professor Aleksandra Zivanovic: A Witch Superior and the Queen of Pentacles, Professor Zivanovic watches over the Witchling Apprentices in the House of Pentacles. Professor Zivanovic is also the princess of the country of Senbrian, a bountiful and abundant land. Jinxy the bunny is her magical familiar.

Professor Jamieson Wolf: Your Hierophant figure, Jamieson Wolf, is a scribe and history professor at the Witchling Academy of Magic. He is a red dragon with the elemental magic of fire.

Professor Lisa Higuchi: A Witch Superior and the Queen of Cups, Professor Higuchi watches over the Witchling Apprentices in the House of Cups. She is caring and creative, and she serves as a motherly figure to the Witchlings in the House of Cups. Her pirate-loving magical familiar is Scullywag the ferret.

Professor Sandra Flores: A Witch Superior and the Queen of Wands, Professor Flores watches over the Witchling Apprentices in the House of Wands. This fun-loving professor guides and watches over the House of Wands with her magical familiar Purrdey, an orange kitty.

Professor Tara Topaz: Professor Topaz teaches potions to beginner Witchling Apprentices. When Charlie failed her potions exam in the Six of Cups, Professor Topaz gave her a second chance by allowing her to retake the exam. Her elemental power is water, and her magical familiar is Simon the hedgehog.

Rina Ito: Rina is the Witchling Apprentice that took third place in the Wands Battle Trial, losing to Ash and Charlie. She lives in the House of Wands, so her elemental power is fire. Jiro, a miniature greyhound, is her magical familiar.

Shadow Witch (also known as Christina McNally): For more than a decade, Witch Christina McNally was possessed by Corrupt Magic. Feared throughout the Light Realm and known as the Shadow Witch, she gained power by stealing magic from Witches and Wizards. She let Corrupt Magic sneak into her heart and soul on her greedy quest for more power. Her elemental magic is air. She is the twin sister of Academy Witch Mistress Maria McNally and Charlie's biological mother. Her magical familiar is the Winged Lion, whom she enslaved.

Water Elemental Goddess: The water elemental goddess is the King of Cups. This goddess loves to party and have a good time. She loves to drop into the celebrations that are held at the House of Cups and sprinkle the Witchlings with good vibes. The elemental power of water was her gift to the realm.

Winged Lion: The only white lion with feathered wings in the Light Realm, he was captured by the Shadow Witch and enslaved as her familiar. This mythical being believed in Charlie and helped her take down the Shadow Witch. He makes his appearance in the Strength card.